ULTIMATE GUIDE TO MASTERING MICROSOFT COPILOT

Unlock the Secrets to Streamlining Your Work with Intelligent Assistance

| AI-Powered Productivity

WisdomBytes Solutions

TABLE OF CONTENTS

CHAPTER 1

INTRODUCTION TO MICROSOFT COPILOT

Microsoft Open AI and Microsoft collaborated to develop Copilot, an artificial intelligence (AI) platform. Its goal is to help developers write code by providing ideas, auto-completion, and code samples. Copilot generates smart code by using machine learning models that have been trained on a large quantity of publicly available code.

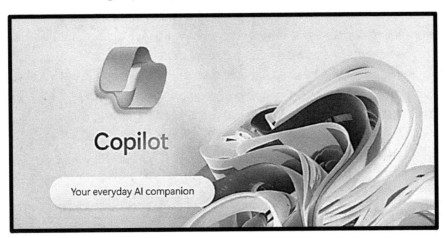

Developers can integrate Copilot into their code tools or Integrated Development Environments (IDEs) to receive suggestions and completions while they write code in real-time. Copilot supports a wide range of programming languages and systems, making it a valuable tool for developers across multiple fields. Copilot aims to increase productivity, reduce repetitive coding jobs, and provide developers with relevant and context-aware code ideas by analyzing the context of the code being written and using its learned models.

Based on the tendencies it has discovered in the training data, it assists in the creation of code snippets, whole lines of code, and even whole functions or classes. It is vital to remember that while Copilot might provide you with useful ideas and code snippets, you should exercise caution when using it. Developers should review the code to ensure that it fits their requirements, follows best practices, and complies with security standards. In principle, Microsoft Copilot aims to be a strong coding assistant that employs AI to accelerate the development process and help engineers create code more quickly.

What is Microsoft Copilot?

Microsoft GitHub and OpenAI collaborated to create Copilot, an AI-powered code completion tool. It was designed to assist developers create code more quickly by proposing code based on context and comments, as well as creating code snippets based on these aspects. To locate useful code snippets, Copilot examines the code environment, which includes the programming language, libraries, and comments. It is built on OpenAI's GPT (Generative Pre-trained Transformer) design, which is also utilized in GPT-3 and other language models.

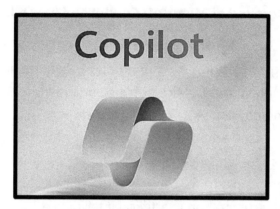

GitHub Copilot is integrated into various popular code editors, including Visual Studio Code, allowing workers to access its features directly from their development environment. It can help you construct functions, complete code blocks, provide documentation, and perform other tasks. It is crucial to remember, however, that while Copilot might be valuable for developers, it is not an alternative to learning to code or designing secure and functional code. Still, developers should double-check the suggestions provided by Copilot to ensure they meet the project's requirements and adhere to best practices.

Also, like with any AI-based tool, Copilot's ideas may not always be correct and may require manual correction or improvement. How Microsoft 365 works Copilot works by merging data from a large language model (LLM) with data securely kept in documents, files, and conversations in your company's Microsoft 365 tenant. Why should you use Copilot with Microsoft 365? Because it can retrieve real-time data from the channels, events, and papers you have access to in M365. The Azure OpenAI service uses free data to develop the huge language model, which is then stored in the Microsoft Cloud. However, Microsoft Graph ensures that you can safely browse your files, papers, and chats. No one else has access to this data, and it is not utilized to teach the AI anything.

History and Development

Microsoft Copilot was made by GitHub, which is a Microsoft Company, and OpenAI working together. It was made possible by improvements in AI technology, especially OpenAI's GPT (Generative Pre-trained Transformer) design, which runs language models like GPT-3.

In brief, here is a background of Microsoft Copilot and how it has changed over time:

- **GitHub Acquisition by Microsoft (2018):** In June 2018, Microsoft acquired GitHub, the largest platform for storing and collaborating on code repositories. This acquisition underscored Microsoft's commitment to supporting open-source communities and developers.
- **Integration of AI Technologies:** Following the acquisition, GitHub began exploring ways to enhance the developer experience by integrating AI technologies into its platform. This initiative led to a collaboration with OpenAI, a leading research organization in artificial intelligence.
- **The emergence of OpenAI's GPT Models:** OpenAI developed several versions of its GPT (Generative Pre-trained Transformer) models, which demonstrated remarkable capabilities in understanding and generating natural language. Trained on vast amounts of internet text data, these models can produce human-like text based on given prompts.
- **Development of the Copilot Concept:** Recognizing the potential of AI to assist developers, GitHub and OpenAI collaborated to create a code completion tool based on GPT technology. The aim was to help developers write code faster and more accurately by providing contextual code suggestions.
- **Testing and Iteration:** Extensive testing and iteration were conducted to enhance Copilot's capabilities and compatibility with various programming languages, tools, and frameworks. GitHub likely engaged with a community of developers to gather feedback and refine the tool during this process.
- **Announcement and Public Release:** Microsoft Copilot was first announced at GitHub's Universe event in June 2021. Initially offered to a select group of users as

a technical preview, Copilot was progressively improved based on user feedback and eventually made available to all GitHub users.

- **Integration with Visual Studio Code:** As part of Microsoft's broader strategy to incorporate AI features into developer tools, Copilot was integrated into Visual Studio Code, one of the most popular code editors used by developers worldwide. This integration enabled developers to leverage Copilot's features directly within their development environment.
- **Continued Development and Improvement:** Since its public release, Microsoft Copilot has continued to evolve and improve. GitHub and OpenAI are likely focused on enhancing the AI model's accuracy, expanding its language support, and addressing any issues or limitations identified by users.

Overall, the creation of Microsoft Copilot is a big step forward in the area where AI and software development meet. The goal is to give workers more power and make the coding process easier by intelligently completing and helping with code.

Key Features

Microsoft Copilot has a few important tools that make coding easier for developers:

- **AI-Powered Code Suggestions:** Copilot leverages advanced machine learning algorithms based on OpenAI's GPT (Generative Pre-trained Transformer) architecture to analyze code context and provide relevant suggestions. It supports numerous programming languages, tools, and frameworks, enabling it to deliver precise and contextually appropriate recommendations.
- **Contextual Code Completion:** Copilot offers intelligent code completion suggestions based on the current context of the code being written. It can generate entire functions, blocks of code, and variable names, significantly reducing the time and effort developers spend on coding.
- **Code Snippet Generation:** Beyond code completion, Copilot can generate entire code snippets based on comments or natural language descriptions provided by developers. This feature is particularly useful for rapidly prototyping solutions or implementing complex methods.
- **Language Support:** Microsoft Copilot supports a wide range of popular programming languages, including JavaScript, Python, Java, C++, and many more.

This extensive language support makes it accessible to developers across various fields and platforms.

- **Integration with Visual Studio Code:** Copilot integrates seamlessly with Visual Studio Code, one of the most popular code editors among developers. This integration allows developers to utilize Copilot's features directly within their development environment, enhancing productivity and workflow efficiency.

- **Code Quality and Best Practices:** Copilot's suggestions are grounded in best coding practices and standard conventions. It helps improve code quality by ensuring consistency, identifying potential errors or bugs, and offering optimized corrections or enhancements.

- **Learning and Collaboration:** As developers use Copilot and incorporate its suggestions into their code, the AI model continues to learn and improve over time. This iterative process fosters a collaborative environment where both developers and the AI benefit from shared insights and knowledge.

- **Accessibility:** Copilot is designed to be beneficial for developers of all skill levels, from beginners to those working on highly complex projects. It provides valuable tips and guidance throughout the coding process, allowing developers to focus on problem-solving and innovation.

- **Security and Privacy:** Microsoft Copilot prioritizes security and privacy by implementing measures to protect sensitive data and code. It adheres to user-defined privacy settings and permissions, ensuring that the generated code snippets do not expose confidential information or violate security policies.

Microsoft Copilot is a productivity tool that uses AI to connect your data across Microsoft Graph and Microsoft 365 services and apps, such as Word, Outlook, Excel, PowerPoint, Teams, and more. Microsoft Copilot uses natural language processing and machine learning techniques to figure out what's going on and make smart suggestions. This means that Copilot has learned from a huge amount of data, which includes code.

These are some of the most important things about Microsoft Copilot for Microsoft 365:

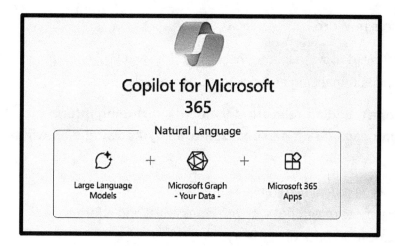

- **Large language models (LLMs)**: Copilot uses LLMs to understand how users behave, look at data, make specific suggestions, give advice, and do things automatically.
- **Integration with Microsoft Graph**: Copilot connects to Microsoft Graph so you can get to your data in Microsoft 365 apps and services.
- **Natural language processing (NLP)**: Natural language processing, or NLP, helps Copilot figure out what the user is trying to say and give them the right answer.
- **Task automation**: Copilot can do things like making reports, arranging meetings, and writing code snippets automatically.
- **Real-time collaboration**: Copilot can help teams work together by giving them ideas and tips in real-time.

Overall, these key features make Microsoft Copilot a useful tool for developers that helps them write code faster, make it better, and work together on software projects more effectively.

Microsoft 365 Copilot Features

There are two ways that Copilot works with Microsoft 365. It works with the user and is built into the Microsoft 365 apps you use every day, like Word, Excel, PowerPoint, Outlook, Teams, etc., to make you more productive, give you better access to data, and generally teach you more.

Here are some of the tools that are known to be part of the Microsoft 365 package with Copilot.

Copilot features in Word.

With Copilot, Word now has the best tool for writing, editing, accessing, adding information, and summarizing as quickly and correctly as possible.

Make a first draft, adding relevant documents, including information that interests you, and giving each task a personalized tone by knowing who will be reading the document.

- Use other text papers to make summaries.
- Suggest styles of writing, such as professional and informal...
- Give reasons to back up a theory.
- Rewrite parts of the text or point out errors.
- Use outlines or frameworks to make drafts of your writing.

Copilot Features in PowerPoint

Copilot in PowerPoint can help you create excellent presentations from your ideas. If you're not particularly creative, Copilot will assist you in telling your stories as effectively as possible. It can convert written documents into entire presentations, replete with fonts and notes to enhance your performance. Alternatively, create a new slideshow from scratch using only an idea or topic. You may shorten long chats with the press of a button, and use your natural language to adjust the style, reformat content, or ensure that animations run in perfect rhythm.

- Use information from another file to make a rough slideshow.
- Summarize presentations.
- Change how a certain slide is laid out.
- Cut down on writing and time it to match animations that are already in a slideshow.

Copilot features in Excel.

Copilot in Excel is designed to make it easier to view and analyze data. Don't be concerned about formulas; instead, ask questions regarding the material provided to obtain real outcomes, correlations, and "what-if" scenarios. It will also employ models to assist you in analyzing your data and offering new approaches to answer your concerns.

To get more information, look for trends, create visualizations, and ask for advice.

- Get rid of the highest or lowest numbers in an **Excel spreadsheet** that is full of data and factors. One good use for this is to see, for example, which groups sell the most items, where the most expensive items are, or which companies sell the most.
- Write up rough bills or books.
- Generate graphs.
- Change one of the factors to assume sales and growth.

Copilot features in Outlook.

Managing our emails takes time which keeps us from being as productive as we could be. We can talk to each other better and faster with Copilot in Outlook. By summarizing long and confusing email threads with many people, you can quickly see what was said, as well as what each person thought and what questions were still unanswered. With a simple prompt, you can reply to an email or turn short notes into clear, defined messages from other Microsoft 365 emails or content you already look at.

- Use information from other papers to write drafts of emails.
- Outline message chains.
- By achieving the above two points, 'clean up' the inbox faster than usual.
- Mark the most important word or item.

Copilot features in Teams.

Copilot in Microsoft Teams enables you to organize more productive meetings, record meeting highlights, and summarize key steps so that everyone on your team understands what to do next. Copilot addresses specific queries or informs you of anything you missed in chat. When you add Copilot to your chats and meetings, you get a powerful tool that may help you with daily activities like creating meeting agendas based on chat history, locating the relevant people to follow up with, and setting up monitoring sessions.

- Make a list of things that you could talk about in meetings.
- Also, make a meeting format based on the chat notes.

- Write up meeting recaps for people who missed it, were late, or just want a summary.

Copilot features in Power Apps.

With Copilot, app developers will be able to collaborate with both robots and humans to produce apps faster and easier. Using natural language models, developers will create apps by having users describe their requirements. Copilot will also allow users to interact with data in the same way they would with a chatbot, making it easier to ask questions and improve analysis.

Power Apps now include built-in robots known as Power Virtual Agents. For developers, this will make it simple to incorporate AI chatbots into their programs. Microsoft aspires to be at the forefront of low-code application development by introducing these technologies. They also seek to develop transformational software in a language that everyone understands.

Copilot Features in Power Automate

Copilot and Create text with GPT are two new features that have been added to Microsoft Power Automate to improve it. When it originally came out in October 2022, the Describe it to Design It feature allowed you to input a simple line and create a procedure based on it. Copilot allows users to improve and adjust flows through AI-powered conversations. Natural language is used to create simple flows and complex corporate operations. Users can ask questions and obtain help making modifications and improvements. Microsoft has also introduced a new function called write text with GPT, which allows users to automatically write material in PC processes. This can save time compared to manual crawling, which is important for customer support, creating daily content, and extracting information from large amounts of text and papers. This implies that these new capabilities make Power Automate smarter, faster, and more effective at automating processes.

Who Can Use Microsoft Copilot?

Microsoft Copilot is an all-in-one system that works for a wide range of users, from individuals and workers to big businesses.

Let's get into the specifics:

- **For Individuals:** Copilot is enjoyable for individuals because it combines fundamental functionality into a unified experience that works across all of your devices. It learns your behaviors on the web, your PC, your apps, and, soon, your phone, so you have the proper abilities when you need them. It's also connected to the internet, so it always has the most recent information. Signing in to Copilot using your Microsoft Entra ID provides you with free business data protection. This implies that chat data is not kept, Microsoft cannot see it and is not utilized to train the models.

- **For Businesses:** Business users can select between Microsoft Copilot or Copilot for Microsoft 365. As previously said, Copilot has numerous commercial benefits, making it an excellent solution for businesses of all sizes. Copilot is an effective tool for increasing productivity and teamwork in enterprises of all kinds, from small start-ups to large multinationals, because it integrates effectively with other Microsoft products. Businesses may tailor Copilot to their needs while keeping data secure and adhering to the rules, thanks to customizable features and user rights.

For Developers:: Copilot's AI-powered features provide developers with a wide range of creative and inventive alternatives. Developers can use Copilot's functionality to manage code jobs, create pictures, and debug. Because it interacts with GitHub, Microsoft Copilot also provides important information for code reviews and advice for improving the quality of your code.

What Are Microsoft's Different Copilots?

Microsoft Copilot is a group of AI-powered assistants that are meant to make different parts of your life more productive and efficient. The image below sorts the different Copilots into groups based on what they can do.

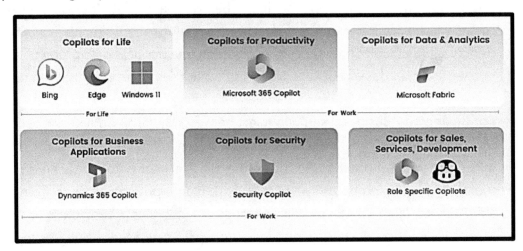

- **Copilots for Life:** You can get Microsoft Copilot (previously Bing Chat or Bing Chat Enterprise) for free. It's ideal for everyday tasks and improves web search and browsing, allowing you to locate what you're looking for faster and more easily. This works excellent for work and play, and it's completely compatible with Windows 11 and Edge.
- **Copilot for Productivity:** Copilot for Microsoft 365 streamlines your processes and helps you get more done in less time by making smart ideas and automating tasks in Microsoft 365 apps like Word, Outlook, and Excel.
- **Data and Analytics Copilots:** These Copilots help you better handle and study your data and can be found in Microsoft Fabric. They give you useful information, help you make choices based on facts, and make your business run more smoothly.
- **Business Applications Copilot:** This Copilot is built for business applications and integrates with Dynamics 365 to improve your company processes and customer interactions. It generates smart ideas and automatically handles tedious tasks, allowing you to focus on what's most essential.
- **Security Copilot:** Microsoft cares a lot about your safety. The Security Copilot has cutting-edge security features that help keep private data safe and in line with regulations.

- **Sales, Services, and Development Copilots:** These are intended to assist with various business functions. Microsoft provides a Copilot for everyone, whether you're a sales professional who wants to increase sales, a service provider who wants to better your service delivery or a developer who wants to make your coding duties easier.

The Microsoft Copilot line includes these and other products that are meant to help you be more productive and efficient. They have many useful features and benefits that make them great for both businesses and people. Let's take a look at each Copilot individually, seeing what makes it special and how it can improve your digital life.

How to Use Microsoft Copilots for Your Everyday Life

Copilot is ready to assist you with projects and daily chores on Bing, Edge, and Windows. AI increases our productivity, creativity, and ability to grasp things. Copilot can help you discover new things whether you're exploring the web, looking for answers, allowing your creativity to flow, or creating helpful material.

Bing: Unleash the Power of AI in Your Searches

Bing Copilot is more than simply a search engine. When you utilize Copilot, it becomes your personal AI assistant for all of your internet searches. Copilot can respond to your inquiries quickly and briefly, saving you time and effort. It also provides ideas and assistance with writing assignments, making it valuable for both students and workers.

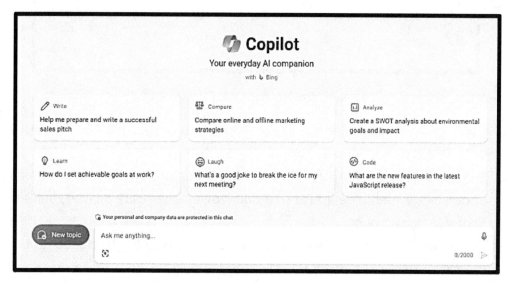

Follow these simple steps to make the most of Bing's Copilot feature. To use Copilot in the search bar, navigate to Bing's home page, sign in with your Microsoft account (or create a free account), and then select "**Search**." Type your question, click "**Enter**," and you'll get quick answers to your inquiries.

Edge: Your Browser Supercharged with AI

Edge is Microsoft's strong and modern web browser, and Copilot enhances it even further. Edge offers AI technologies that can help you find things faster, improve your viewing experience, and protect your online data. It also works seamlessly with Bing to provide you with a comprehensive and rapid search experience.

Follow these easy steps to learn how to turn on Copilot in Edge.

- Open your Microsoft Edge browser. It can be downloaded from the Microsoft website if you don't already have it.
- Ensure your Microsoft Account is signed in. If not, use the three-dot button in the upper right corner to get to Settings and Profiles. Then, click on Add Profile to sign in or make an account.
- In the top right corner of the browser window, click on the three dots to bring up the menu. This will open the Edge Settings.

- Go to the Settings menu and click on **Privacy**, search, and services.
- In the Services list, scroll down and click on Microsoft Copilot.
- To use **Copilot**, flip the switch to "**On**."

Copilot will make your Edge viewing better by giving you smart ideas and faster search results. Remember that you need to have the most recent version of Edge installed for Copilot to work properly. Regular changes add new features and make sure that your online experience is as safe as possible.

Copilot for Windows11: AI on Your Desktop

Begin a revolution in efficiency with Copilot for Windows 11, a cutting-edge AI-powered assistant that will improve your digital life. Copilot is a smart assistant. It integrates seamlessly into your workflow and may be accessed via the taskbar or by hitting Win+C on your computer. You'll be more productive since Copilot makes it simple to locate answers and ideas on the internet, fostering innovation and teamwork. Its basic support will allow you to think less and complete your tasks faster. Copilot simplifies hard tasks by optimizing procedures, making your daily life go more easily.

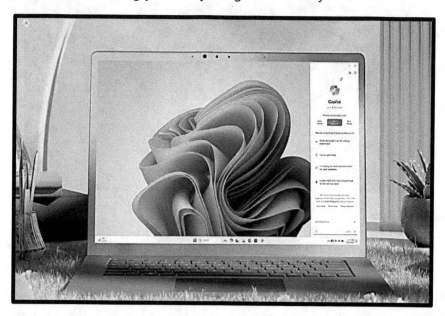

Copilot is with you on all screen sizes, whether you're at work, school, or home, helping you with your apps. It helps you concentrate and gets things done faster when it's around.

The Role of AI in Modern Workspaces

"AI is not just a technology; it's an opportunity for humanity to redefine what's possible." AI has evolved into a potent force that is altering a wide range of industries and our work practices. There's no doubting that it has transformed settings, transforming the ordinary office into a smart and evolving ecology.

Enhanced Productivity and Efficiency

"AI is not just a technology; it's an opportunity for humanity to redefine what's possible." AI has evolved into a potent force that is altering a wide range of industries and our work practices. There's no doubting that it has transformed settings, transforming the ordinary office into a smart and evolving ecology.

Intelligent Decision-Making

When artificial intelligence is utilized to evaluate data, organizations may make smarter decisions. Advanced algorithms can swiftly sort through large amounts of data, identify trends, and generate relevant insights. From anticipating market trends to enhancing supply chain management, AI provides business executives with the tools they need to make smarter decisions with greater confidence and accuracy.

Personalized Experiences

AI-driven systems can provide more tailored experiences for both employees and customers. In offices, AI may learn what each employee prefers, adjust based on their activities, and tailor the environment to their needs. AI makes individualized learning and training programs, as well as flexible work conditions, more exciting and rewarding for employees. This increases their productivity and happiness.

Augmented Collaboration

AI technologies make it easy for people from different teams and departments to work together and talk to each other. Intelligent virtual assistants and robots make it easier to share information in real-time and make work easier. AI-powered collaboration tools make it easy for teams in different places to work together, removing geographical hurdles and creating a more welcoming workplace.

Job Transformations and Skill Development

Adding AI to workspaces will always alter the jobs that people perform. Even if some tedious duties are automated, new employment and opportunities emerge. Companies will require individuals who possess new skills such as AI proficiency, critical thinking, and creativity. Employee upskilling and reskilling programs are required to provide them with the necessary skills to succeed in an AI-driven workplace.

Today, AI plays many roles in the workplace, and these roles are changing quickly. Here are a few important ways that AI is changing and improving modern workplaces:

1. **Automation of Repetitive Tasks:** AI technologies such as robotic process automation (RPA) and machine learning are increasingly being employed in a variety of fields to manage repetitive operations. This covers tasks such as data input, document management, customer service, and more. By automating these repetitive operations, employees may focus on more critical and creative aspects of their occupations.

2. **Enhanced Decision-Making:** AI-powered analytics and decision support solutions assist enterprises in making more informed data-driven decisions. These systems can analyze large amounts of data, identify patterns and trends, and provide information to help you make informed decisions. AI-driven analytics are critical

for better company performance since they help with anything from targeted marketing campaigns to simplifying the supply chain.

3. **Natural Language Processing (NLP) for Communication:** Virtual assistants, chatbots, and language translation systems that let individuals within and outside of enterprises communicate with one another are powered by AI-driven NLP technologies. Chatbots and other virtual assistants can answer basic questions, schedule meetings, and provide information to employees. This makes contact easier and increases productivity.

4. **Personalized Experiences:** AI enables workers and shoppers to have unique experiences. In human resources, for example, AI may analyze employee data to ensure that learning and development programs are personalized to each individual's needs. Similarly, AI-powered recommendation engines can help buyers identify the perfect products based on their previous purchases and behaviors.

5. **Improved Customer Service:** Chatbots and virtual assistants driven by AI are altering the way customer service is delivered by providing support 24 hours a day, seven days a week, answering common inquiries, and resolving problems quickly. These AI systems are good at answering a lot of queries fast, allowing human agents to do more difficult and useful work.

6. **Predictive Maintenance:** In manufacturing and other industries, AI-powered predictive maintenance systems analyze sensor data to forecast when equipment may fail. Companies can reduce downtime, maintenance costs, and business inefficiencies by identifying potential issues early on.

7. **Augmented Creativity:** AI tools are increasingly being utilized to assist individuals be more creative in fields such as writing, design, and music production. AI-powered tools can assist developers in coming up with ideas, creating content planning, and even producing text for them. Similarly, AI may help artists by generating new designs based on the parameters they provide.

8. **Remote Work Enablement:** As more people opt to work from home, AI technologies are critical for making it easier for them to collaborate, communicate, and accomplish tasks in virtual places. Collaboration tools, virtual meeting helpers, and AI-powered project management platforms enable remote teams to stay in touch and organized.

9. **Ethical and Bias Mitigation:** As AI technologies grow increasingly ubiquitous in the workplace, there is a greater emphasis on ensuring their honest and ethical use. More and more firms are investing in AI ethical models, technologies that detect bias, and diversity programs to ensure that AI algorithms and decision-making processes are not biased.

Overall, AI is transforming modern workplaces by automating chores, facilitating decision-making, boosting communication, personalizing circumstances, allowing people to work from home, and increasing creativity. As AI advances, it is likely to have a greater impact on the workplace, making it more efficient, innovative, and competitive. However, it is vital to deal with issues like ethics, bias, and privacy to ensure that AI tools are utilized in the workplace responsibly and ethically.

Impact of Microsoft Copilot on Daily Workflows

Microsoft Copilot could have a big impact on workers' daily work by making it easier to code, making them more productive, and making it easier for people to work together.

Here are some ways that Copilot can change the way people do their daily work:

1. **Efficient Code Completion:** Copilot makes smart code completion suggestions based on what the user is currently writing. This can save time for developers by typing bits of code that are used repeatedly, such as import statements, function descriptions, and variable declarations.
2. **Faster Prototyping:** Copilot can generate entire sections of code based on what the programmer says or types in natural language. This feature enables developers to quickly prototype solutions, allowing them to test ideas and make modifications without having to create completely new code.
3. **Learning and Knowledge Sharing:** Copilot's ideas are based on a vast amount of code from various sources, including open-source libraries. The more developers use and implement Copilot's recommendations, the more they will learn about new coding methodologies, tools, and best practices. This motivates development teams to continue learning and sharing what they know.
4. **Code Quality Improvement:** Copilot's ideas are based on best practices and standard ways of writing code. Copilot can help improve code quality, consistency, and maintainability across projects by making ideas that follow coding standards.

5. **Reduced Cognitive Load:** Copilot can assist developers navigate difficult codebases by providing context-based suggestions and code examples. This reduces the mental strain that comes with understanding code you don't know and speeds up the process of solving problems or making changes.

6. **Collaboration Enhancement:** Copilot can help team members work together by giving them consistent code advice and tips. Developers can use Copilot's ideas to make their coding styles and methods more consistent, which will make code reviews and merging go more smoothly.

7. **Accessibility and Inclusivity:** Copilot can assist developers at all levels, even those who are just learning how to code. Copilot can help people with diverse backgrounds and experiences contribute more successfully to software development activities by providing helpful guidance and assistance throughout the writing process.

8. **Integration with Development Environments:** Copilot works perfectly with popular code editors like Visual Studio Code, so workers can use its features right from the programming environment they prefer. With this integration, Copilot fits right into workers' current processes, so they don't have to switch between tools.

Overall, Microsoft Copilot has the potential to revolutionize the way developers work by removing tedious processes, allowing them to create rapid prototypes, improving code quality, fostering teamwork, and giving people of all skill levels more power. Because employees are already utilizing Copilot in their daily work, its effect on productivity and innovative ideas in software development is likely to grow with time.

Use Cases That Make a Real Difference

These are some real-life things that Microsoft Copilot can do for you and your business. What's important is not so much the features and duties as the value they can bring.

1. **Kickstart Creativity**: Stop looking at blank Word pages. Copilot provides a rough draft, allowing you to focus on improving your ideas. It becomes easier and more natural to use PowerPoint presentations and Excel studies. You may have heard about ChatGPT. This is a creative AI that helps you shape your thoughts into a great starting point for whatever project you're working on.

2. **Boost Productivity:** Prepare to tackle your bothersome email and make the most of each meeting. Copilot highlights meeting action points in real-time, summarizes long email chains, and provides recommendations for how to respond. It's surprising how quickly those tiny tasks that take five minutes here and there accumulate. This is no longer essential with Copilot.

3. **Low Code:** Have you ever felt that Microsoft 365 apps had too many functions for you to manage? We aren't brave enough to deal with Access, let's face it. Users will be able to use platforms that are difficult to understand because of Copilot's natural language orders. This will make them easier to use and provide them with more opportunities to make their work valuable.

4. **Always Learning:** Copilot isn't set and forgotten. Like any good learning model, it's made to change and adapt to new jobs and ways of doing things and to help you with whatever you're doing in general. This means it should live up to its name over time.

5. **Responsible AI:** Microsoft is clearly committed to responsible AI development. The organization adheres to a strong AI standard that safeguards data privacy, limits harmful content, and ensures that everyone is treated fairly. This ensures that the AI system's decisions are understandable and promotes user freedom and control. There has been a lot of talk about how algorithms can make it difficult to utilize social media sites, so it's fantastic to see Microsoft taking the next stage in computing seriously.

Supported Programming Languages

It works with many programming languages, like Python, JavaScript, TypeScript, C++, and more. It can be used by a lot of different developers because of this.

Differences between Copilot AI and other Virtual Assistants

Other virtual assistants, like Siri, Alexa, and Google Assistant, are very different from Microsoft Copilot AI in terms of what they can do and who they are meant for.

These are some important differences:

1. **Target Audience:**
   - **Microsoft Copilot AI:** Microsoft Copilot is primarily designed for developers and is intended to help them write code faster. It provides ideas for how to complete writing code, generates code snippets, and helps you comprehend what you're doing while you're writing it.
   - **Other Virtual Assistants:** Virtual assistants like Siri, Alexa, Google Assistant, and others like them are made for regular people and can do a lot of things, like play music, set notes, handle smart home devices, give you weather updates, and answer general questions.

2. **Scope of Assistance:**
   - **Microsoft Copilot AI:** Copilot's primary responsibility is to assist developers with coding tasks. It proposes methods to finish portions of code, develops code snippets from natural language descriptions, and provides relevant support based on the code being written.
   - **Other Virtual Assistants:** General-purpose virtual assistants like Siri, Alexa, and Google Assistant can help with a broader range of tasks, such as managing personal duties, acquiring information from the internet, controlling smart home devices, sending messages, making calls, creating reminders, and demonstrating how to navigate.

3. **Contextual Understanding:**
   - **Microsoft Copilot AI:** Copilot learned about programming languages, tools, and coding standards by reviewing a large quantity of code from many sources. It leverages this information to provide the developer with code suggestions and assistance that are relevant to their needs.
   - **Other Virtual Assistants:** General-purpose Virtual assistants can grasp orders and questions written in everyday English, but they do not understand the context as effectively as Copilot does. They obey pre-set orders and replies and may not be as good at certain activities, such as software production.

4. **Integration with Development Tools:**
   - **Microsoft Copilot:** Microsoft Copilot is built into famous code editors like Visual Studio Code, so developers can use its features right from their working

environment. This tight connection makes things easier for developers and makes sure that workflows work well together.

- **Other Virtual Assistants:** You can usually get to general-purpose virtual assistants through their apps or devices, like smartphones and smart speakers, and they might not be directly built into development environments or tools.

5. **Learning and Improvement:**
   - **Microsoft Copilot AI:** Copilot continues to learn and improve over time as a result of developer feedback and the code it uses. As developers use Copilot and provide input, the AI model changes and improves its ability to provide meaningful and accurate ideas.
   - **Other Virtual Assistants:** General-purpose virtual assistants also learn and get better over time, but they learn more about what users want, how to better understand language, and how to give better answers to general questions and tasks.

To summarize, Copilot AI and other virtual assistants use AI technologies, but they are used for different purposes, target different groups of people, and have distinct qualities that are unique to respective industries. Copilot was created to help engineers write code faster and more efficiently. Other virtual assistants are more general-use and offer a broader range of functions for personal and domestic duties.

CHAPTER 2

GETTING STARTED

It's pretty easy to get started with Microsoft Copilot, especially if you already know how to code and use code editors like Visual Studio Code.

If you want to learn how to use Microsoft Copilot, here are the steps:

1. **Install Visual Studio Code (VS Code):** If you haven't already, get Visual Studio Code and install it. It's one of the code editors that Copilot can work with.

2. **Install the GitHub Copilot Extension:** Once Visual Studio Code is installed, you will need to download the GitHub Copilot extension. To access the Extensions view, open Visual Studio Code and select the square button in the sidebar, or press Ctrl+Shift+X (Windows/Linux) or Cmd+Shift+X (Mac). Find "GitHub Copilot" in the Extensions Marketplace, and click "Install" to add the add-on.

3. **Sign in to GitHub:** You'll need to use your GitHub account to sign in to Microsoft Copilot. You will need to make a GitHub account if you don't already have one. Sign in to Visual Studio Code with your GitHub account after making an account or logging in if you already have one.

4. **Set Up GitHub Copilot:** After downloading the app and logging in, you'll need to set up GitHub Copilot. To conclude the setup, simply follow the on-screen directions. Typically, this entails providing them access to your GitHub account and configuring any additional settings that are required.

5. **Start Coding with Copilot:** After you've loaded and configured GitHub Copilot, you may begin using it to help you write code. Start typing code in Visual Studio Code by opening a code file, either new or old. Copilot will provide you with code ideas and completions based on what you're typing.

Setting up Microsoft Copilot

Setting up Microsoft Copilot can be fun and useful as well! Now let's begin. To help you through the process, here are some steps:

1. **Installation**:

- First, make sure that your computer has a code editor that is compatible with it. Visual Studio Code (VS Code) is officially supported by Microsoft Copilot.
- Open VS Code and press Ctrl+Shift+X to go to the Extensions Marketplace.
- Look for "Copilot" and install the "GitHub Copilot" app.
- Do what it says to do to log in with your GitHub account.

2. **Authentication**:
   - After installing the app, you'll need to sign in with your GitHub credentials.
   - Click on the GitHub Copilot button in the sidebar of VS Code, then follow the on-screen prompts to sign in.

3. **Configuration**:
   - Click on the gear button in the GitHub Copilot panel to change how Copilot works for you.
   - Change settings like language support, key bindings, and how snippets work.

4. **Usage**:
   - Open an old code project or start a new one.
   - As you write code, Copilot will give you ideas, autocomplete words, and even make up whole functions based on what you're writing.
   - Press Tab or Enter to agree with Copilot's ideas.

5. **Learning and Feedback**:
   - Copilot changes as you use it and learn from the way you code.
   - If you have any problems or suggestions, you could report them through the app or the GitHub source.

Keep in mind that Copilot is a powerful tool, but it's important to understand the code it creates and fix anything wrong.

System Requirements and Installation

Microsoft recently expanded the availability of Copilot, its conversational AI assistant, to additional Windows 10 customers. The aim appears to be to let customers who are still using Windows 10 or have devices that are incompatible with Windows 11 try out the AI helper. It's worth noting that at the time of writing, 69 percent of Windows-based PC users fall into this category.

Accessing and participating in the program is just the beginning. People who want to utilize Copilot must also make sure their laptops match specific requirements. To accomplish this, you'll need at least 4GB of RAM and a display adapter capable of at least 720p quality. The preview is only available in select locations, including North America, some portions of Asia, and some sections of South America.

There are currently no plans to expand its availability. Other minor limitations for Copilot on Windows 10 include the inability to function with taskbars on the left or right side of the screen, the inability to support setups with multiple monitors, and the inability to grant access to Pro machines managed by groups. The feature is accessible via an icon on the right side of the taskbar for Windows 10 users.

It can be used to answer queries, generate new ideas, control Windows features, work with papers, and so on. Once Copilot is ready, users can activate it by pressing the button on the right side of the window. Copilot allows users to ask inquiries, operate Windows programs, and interact with documents.

It functions a little differently on Windows 10 because it lacks several Windows 11 features, but it still has many AI-powered features. Microsoft Copilot was a plugin for Visual Studio Code, a popular code editor. Here are the general system prerequisites and steps for setting it up:

System Requirements

1. **Operating System**:

   - Windows 10 or 11 (64-bit)
   - macOS 10.13+
   - Linux

2. **Visual Studio Code**:

   - Version 1.61.0 or later.

3. **Internet Connection**:

   - You need a stable internet connection because Microsoft Copilot uses cloud-based models.

4. **Subscription Plans**:

- **To buy Microsoft Copilot for Microsoft 365, you need to have one of the following subscription plans:**

  - Microsoft 365 E5

  - Microsoft 365 E3

  - Office 365 E3

  - Office 365 E5

  - Microsoft 365 Business Standard

  - Microsoft 365 Business Premium

  - Microsoft 365 A5 for faculty*

  - Microsoft 365 A3 for faculty*

  - Office 365 A5 for faculty*

  - Office 365 A3 for faculty*

Note: People who have an Education or Business plan that doesn't include Teams can still buy Copilot licenses.

5. **Base Licenses**:
   - For your users to get a Copilot for Microsoft 365 license, they must already have one of the base licenses listed above.
   - Plans like Microsoft 365 E5, E3, Office 365 E3, E5, and others that meet the requirements are needed.

6. **Microsoft 365 Apps**:

   - Desktop apps from Microsoft 365, like Word, Excel, PowerPoint, Outlook, and Teams, need to be set up.
   - Once a license is given, Copilot will also be available in the web versions of the apps.

7. **OneDrive Account**:
   - To use some parts of Copilot for Microsoft 365, like restoring files and managing OneDrive, users need to have a OneDrive account.

8. **Outlook for Windows**:
   - Use the new Outlook (Windows, Mac, Web, and Mobile) for smooth integration. Classic Outlook (Windows) can also be used with Copilot.
9. **Microsoft Teams**:
   - Use the Teams PC client or web client to use Copilot in Microsoft Teams. It works with both the old and new versions of Teams.

Before you install, you should make sure of the following:

Purchase Licenses

- Acquire Copilot for Microsoft 365 licenses through the Microsoft 365 admin center, Microsoft partners, or the Microsoft account team.

Assign Licenses

- Allocate Copilot licenses to eligible users based on their existing base licenses.

Configure OneDrive

- Ensure users have OneDrive accounts to enable Copilot to function optimally.

Set Up Outlook

- For the best Copilot experience, use the new Outlook. However, the classic version of Outlook is also supported.

Enable Copilot in Teams

- Download the Teams desktop app or log in to the web app.
- Copilot is available in Teams on Windows, Mac, the web, Android, and iOS.

Remember that Copilot helps you be more productive and creative by giving you clever assistance in real-time.

Installation Process

1. **Install Visual Studio Code**: Get Visual Studio Code from the official page and install it if you haven't already.

2. **Open Visual Studio Code**: Open Visual Studio Code after it's been installed.

3. **Install Microsoft Copilot Extension**:

   - To get to the Extensions view in Visual Studio Code, press **Ctrl+Shift+X** or click on the square button on the left.
   - Navigate to the Extensions Marketplace and look for "GitHub Copilot" or "Microsoft Copilot."
   - Select the "Install" button next to the add-on for Microsoft Copilot.
4. **Authenticate with GitHub** (if required): You may need to sign in to Copilot with your GitHub account. To verify, just do what it says.

5. **Set up Copilot**: Once Copilot is installed, it may ask you to set up some options or settings. As instructed, follow the steps given.

6. **Restart Visual Studio Code** (if required): Sometimes, after installing an application, Visual Studio Code needs to be restarted. If asked, start the editor up again.

7. **Start Using Copilot**: Once Copilot is installed and set up, you should see ideas and assistance from it while you code in languages that it supports.

Integration with GitHub

Microsoft Copilot integrates seamlessly with GitHub, the world's largest platform for storing and collaboratively working on code repositories. This integration facilitates developers' work on their projects by incorporating Copilot's AI-powered code completion and recommendation features into the GitHub environment. **This is how Copilot and GitHub work together:**

1. **GitHub Copilot Extension:** Copilot is available as an add-on for Visual Studio Code, one of the most popular code tools used by developers. Developers can use the functionality of the Copilot extension directly from their working environment after installing it.

2. **Code Completion and Suggestions:** When developers are writing code in VS Code with the Copilot extension enabled, Copilot provides intelligent code completion suggestions and code snippets relevant to the current circumstance as

29

they write code. These thoughts are generated by looking at the code, notes, and the developer's natural language explanations.

3. **GitHub Repository Integration:** To teach its AI model, Copilot uses GitHub's huge collection of open-source code. Copilot can make correct code ideas based on the computer language, libraries, and frameworks being used in a project by looking at trends and examples from GitHub repositories.

4. **GitHub Co-pilot Mode:** Copilot's relationship to GitHub extends beyond simply finishing programming in VS programming. In "GitHub Copilot" mode, developers can collaborate with Copilot directly in GitHub's web-based code editor while browsing files on the site. In this mode, developers can easily create code snippets, comment descriptions, and even full functions directly from the GitHub interface.

5. **Learning and Improvement:** The AI model continues to learn and improve over time when developers utilize Copilot and follow its advice. When Copilot provides code ideas, it uses input from developers and continuing research of code patterns and trends on GitHub to make them more accurate and valuable.

6. **Community Feedback and Collaboration:** GitHub allows developers to discuss Copilot's ideas and collaborate to make them better. Users can immediately submit bugs, issues, and feature requests to the GitHub Copilot source. This allows the tool to continuously improve.

Overall, integrating Copilot with GitHub makes it easier for developers to create code by providing AI-powered code completion and recommendation tools within their work environment and GitHub repositories. This combination simplifies the process of writing code, increases production, and encourages developers to collaborate.

GitHub Copilot Integration

1. **Installation**:
   - To use Copilot with GitHub, you have to add the **GitHub Copilot extension** to your code editor. Visual Studio Code currently supports this.
   - Open VS Code, press Ctrl+Shift+X to open the Extensions Marketplace, and look for "GitHub Copilot." Install the extension and follow any steps for logging in.

2. **Authentication**:
   - Once the app is installed, sign in with your GitHub account.

- Click on the GitHub Copilot button in the sidebar of VS Code, then follow the on-screen prompts to sign in.

3. **Configuration**:
   - Click the gear button in the GitHub Copilot panel to change how Copilot works for you.
   - Change settings like language support, key bindings, and how snippets work.

4. **Usage**:
   - Open an old code project or start a new one.
   - As you write code, Copilot will make smart suggestions, complete your code automatically, and even make up whole functions based on what you're writing.
   - Press **Tab or Enter** to agree with Copilot's ideas.

5. **Learning and Feedback**:
   - Copilot changes as you use it and learn from the way you code.
   - If you have any problems or suggestions, you could report them through the app or the GitHub source.

Using Copilot in Various Development Environments

Visual Studio Code (VS Code), one of the most popular code editors used by developers, is integrated with Microsoft Copilot. However, there could be variations in how well Copilot functions with other coding platforms. **Here are some ways to use Copilot in different working environments:**

1. **Visual Studio Code (VS Code):** The GitHub Copilot app makes it simple to use Copilot with Visual Studio Code. After adding the Copilot app to VS Code, you can use its functionalities directly from the code editor. As you write code in VS Code, Copilot provides you with code ideas, completions, and guidance based on what you're doing.

2. **GitHub Repository:** Copilot also offers a mode called "GitHub Copilot" that allows you to collaborate with Copilot directly in GitHub's web-based code editor while reading GitHub projects. In this mode, you can create code snippets, comment explanations, and even full functions directly from the GitHub interface.

3. **Other Development Environments:** Copilot works best with VS Code and GitHub, although you may be able to use some of its features in other programming environments, albeit not as simply. You can use Copilot's concepts by copying and

pasting code snippets created in VS Code into other IDEs or tools. However, the Copilot program may not function as well in other environments as it does in VS Code because it is fully integrated and operates without any problems.

4. **API and Integration Possibilities:** In the future, Copilot may be able to connect to other development platforms via APIs or links built by outside developers, or it may receive official support from GitHub and Microsoft. Keep an eye on GitHub and Microsoft's updates and announcements to see what changes in this area.

Overall, Copilot's main integrations are with VS Code and GitHub. However, developers may still be able to use its features in other development environments by copying and pasting code snippets manually or by waiting for possible future extensions and mergers.

Privacy and Security Considerations

When using an AI-powered tool, such as Microsoft Copilot, you need to consider privacy and security. Microsoft provides numerous choices for protecting your information. Microsoft is dedicated to privacy, security, compliance, and responsible AI practices, which is how all Copilot for Security data is handled. Microsoft's approved procedures control who has access to the systems that keep your data. **When using Copilot, here are some important things to keep in mind about privacy and safety:**

1. **Data Privacy:** To generate code ideas, Copilot examines a large quantity of code from a variety of sources. It was trained on public code files, but if you're working with private or sensitive code, be mindful of how this may compromise privacy. When using Copilot, do not give out confidential information or secret codes.

2. **Data Security:** Make sure your development environment is secure and up to date with the most recent security patches and fixes. This applies to any code tools or integrated development environments (IDEs) that you use with Copilot. For increased safety, this helps prevent potential security weaknesses that bad people could employ.

3. **Code Privacy:** Be careful when you use Copilot to make code snippets that could hold private data or secret methods. Before sharing the created code, make sure it is clean and free of bugs, especially if it contains private or secret logic.

4. **Access Controls:** Make sure there are access restrictions in place to limit who can use Copilot and prevent unauthorized use. If you work with others, be sure that

everyone on your team knows how to use Copilot and that only authorized team members can access it.

5. **User Consent and Transparency:** Allowing users to provide consent and being transparent about how their data is used: Read and understand Copilot's data usage and privacy policies. The regulations on GitHub specify how data is gathered and used using Copilot. Users should read these policies to make informed decisions about how to use the product.

6. **Feedback and Reporting:** If you have any privacy or security concerns while using Copilot, you should notify GitHub or Microsoft in the appropriate way. Let the creators know about any faults or vulnerabilities you notice so they can make the tool safer and more private overall.

7. **Regular Updates:** Make sure you are aware of Copilot modifications and security fixes, and that you are using the most recent version of the tool. Update your working environment and any software that works with it on a regular basis to eliminate security concerns and make the most of the newest features and modifications.

If developers follow these privacy and security guidelines, they will be able to use Microsoft Copilot more successfully while decreasing data privacy and security risks. When utilizing Copilot or any other AI-powered technology, it's crucial to stay vigilant and take action to solve any privacy or security risks that may arise.

Initial Configuration best

Making the best settings for Microsoft Copilot means making sure it's set up to improve your coding experience while also taking privacy, security, and personal tastes into account. **Here is a list of the best ways to set up Microsoft Copilot for the first time:**

1. **Install Visual Studio Code (VS Code):** Make sure that VS Code is already set up on your computer. Copilot is built into VS Code, so you need to have this code editor loaded to use Copilot's functions.

2. **Install GitHub Copilot Extension:** You can get the GitHub Copilot extension from the Visual Studio Code Marketplace and install it. To do this, press Ctrl+Shift+X to open the Extensions view and look for "GitHub Copilot." Then, choose the extension and select "Install."

3. **Sign in to GitHub:** Sign into your GitHub account in Visual Studio Code. To access the command line, press Ctrl+Shift+P or click the GitHub button in the sidebar. Enter "GitHub: Sign In" and then follow the on-screen prompts to log in. This step is important to access Copilot's features because it trains its AI model using the code sources from GitHub.

4. **Configure Copilot Settings:** Copilot has various parameters that you can adjust to make it act the way you want. To access the Copilot options, click on the gear icon in the lower left corner of VS Code and select "**Settings**". Type "**Copilot**" into the settings search field to limit the settings related to Copilot. Look over the options and make any adjustments you believe are required depending on your preferences.

5. **Explore Copilot Features:** Take some time to get to know Copilot's features and capabilities. Try typing notes, code snippets, or natural language descriptions to discover how Copilot can help you write code and generate ideas. Try utilizing Copilot in various writing jobs to discover how it can help you get things done faster.

6. **Learn Keyboard Shortcuts:** To get more done with Copilot, learn the keyboard shortcuts that work with it. To use Copilot's ideas, press Ctrl+Space (on Windows) or Cmd+Space (on macOS).

7. **Review Privacy and Security Settings:** Check Copilot's privacy and security settings to ensure you understand how your information is being used and stored. GitHub provides explicit information on how Copilot gathers and uses data, and you can verify and update your privacy settings as necessary.

8. **Provide Feedback:** As you use Copilot, you might want to tell GitHub and Microsoft what you think so they can make it more accurate and useful. You can give comments right in VS Code or through the feedback methods on GitHub.

By following these best practices for initial setup, you can set up Microsoft Copilot correctly and change how it works to fit your coding needs and preferences. Keep up with Copilot's updates and improvements, and make changes to your setup as needed to get the most out of your writing experience.

CHAPTER 3

UNDERSTANDING COPILOT SUGGESTIONS

1. **Input Prompt and Grounding**:
   - Before using Microsoft 365 Copilot, you must answer a certain question. You tell them what you need, such as composing an email, creating a report, or writing code for a function.
   - • Grounding allows for magical experiences. The copilot takes your cue and improves it by adding more depth and awareness of the circumstance. This procedure ensures that the answers you receive are meaningful and relevant to your job.

2. **Privacy and Security**:
   - • Copilot is concerned about your safety. The fact that it connects to your organization's data in Microsoft 365 protects sensitive information.
   - • The tool leverages Microsoft Graph to analyze your data rather than directly accessing it. This group includes letters, conversations, and papers. It's crucial to remember that Copilot's large language models (LLMs) are saved in the Microsoft Cloud and not trained on your company's data. Your privacy is intact.

3. **Policy Adherence**:
   - • Copilot follows your company's security, compliance, and privacy regulations established in Microsoft 365. It follows the rules!
   - •Every discourse begins from scratch. Your chat information has been wiped, so your chats with others will not accidentally teach the LLMs anything.

4. **Capabilities and Efficiency**:
   - Copilot provides answers based on the information you provide. It's like having an extremely smart person help you write.
   - Use Microsoft Search to rapidly catch up and save time.
   - Additionally, Copilot reads crucial data from OneNote, Word, or PowerPoint files, which is a terrific method to begin generating new content.

How Copilot Works

Advanced machine learning models, especially the GPT (Generative Pre-trained Transformer) design, are used by Microsoft Copilot to look at the context of code and make smart code ideas.

This is how Copilot works in brief:

1. **Training Data:** Copilot is trained on a large collection of code from many sources, including GitHub's open-source files. This dataset contains a wide variety of computer languages, libraries, systems, and techniques for producing code. This big set of various datasets helps Copilot learn about common code trends, idioms, and best practices.

2. **GPT Architecture:** Copilot is based on Opening AI's GPT design. The acronym GPT stands for "Generative Pre-trained Transformer." GPT is a cutting-edge language model that leverages self-attention to interpret input and generate text that appears to be authored by a person. Copilot's use of code-specific data to fine-tune its model makes it highly good at comprehending and producing code samples.

3. **Contextual Understanding:** When you write code or natural language descriptions in your code editor, Copilot scans the surrounding variable names, function signatures, notes, and other code snippets. It makes advantage of this contextual knowledge to generate useful code ideas that are appropriate for the current coding circumstance.

4. **Code Completion and Generation:** Copilot suggests how to finish off function names, variable names, method calls, and other forms of code based on what you're doing. Copilot may even generate entire chunks of code from notes or natural language descriptions provided by the coder. These snippets of code are created using the patterns and structures that were learned from training data.

5. **Machine Learning Models:** The machine learning models in Copilot are constantly learning and adapting based on how users engage with them and what they say. The models become smarter as developers utilize Copilot and incorporate its suggestions into their code. Over time, these interactions improve the models' predictions. This process of learning over and over helps Copilot get better at recommending code and being correct about it.

6. **Privacy and Security:** Because of concerns about privacy and security, Copilot operates in a manner that respects privacy. It does not communicate or save user data or code outside of the local development region. Copilot's training data originates from public code sources. Unless the user explicitly requests it to, it does not read or investigate confidential or sensitive code.

Microsoft Copilot primarily employs machine learning to comprehend code context, generate smart code suggestions, and assist developers in writing code more quickly. It is a handy tool for improving the writing experience. It can look at different code styles and alter them based on how the user interacts with it.

How does Microsoft Copilot for Microsoft 365 work?

The features of Microsoft Copilot for Microsoft 365 that users see in Microsoft 365 Apps and other places look like smart features, functions, and the ability to remind users. The foundation **LLMs and Microsoft-only technologies work together to make a system that lets you view, use, and control your organization's data safely.**

- **Microsoft 365**. Word, Excel, PowerPoint, Outlook, Teams, and Loop integrate with Copilot for Microsoft 365 to assist users with their work. For example, Word's Copilot feature is designed to assist users in creating, reading, and editing documents. For the same reason, Copilot in other apps assists users with their work in those apps.
- **Microsoft Copilot with Graph-grounded chat** lets you use work-related material and context in chats in Microsoft Copilot. You can draft content, catch up on what you missed, and get answers to questions through open-ended prompts with Graph-grounded chat, all while keeping your work data safe.
- **Microsoft Graph** has been a key component of Microsoft 365 for a long time. There is information on how users, actions, and your organization's data are related. Using the Microsoft Graph API, you may add more information from customer signs like emails, chats, papers, and meetings to the prompt.
- **Semantic Index** for Copilot uses several LLMs that sit on top of Microsoft Graph to understand user questions and give you smart, useful, and international answers that make you more productive. You can quickly look through billions of vectors,

which are mathematical representations of features or characteristics, to find information that is useful to your company.

Looking at the image below will help you understand how Microsoft Copilot for Microsoft 365 works.

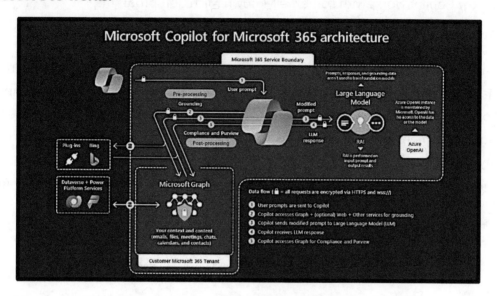

To explain how Microsoft Copilot for Microsoft 365 works, read on:

- Users can instruct Copilot to perform a task in apps such as Word or PowerPoint.
- Furthermore, Copilot pre-processes the input prompt using a technique known as "grounding," which improves its specificity. This helps you acquire responses that are relevant and valuable to your job. The prompt may include text from input files as well as other items discovered by Copilot. It is subsequently sent to the LLM for processing. Copilot can only view data that a specific user has access to, such as through role-based access rules in Microsoft 365.
- After receiving the LLM's response, Copilot processes it. This post-processing includes calls to Microsoft Graph for grounding, responsible AI checks, security, compliance, and privacy reviews, as well as command creation.
- Copilot returns the answer to the app so that the user can review it and decide what to do with it.

How does Copilot work with Each Microsoft Application?

Copilot is a powerful tool that is meant to work as smoothly as possible with other Microsoft products. It helps users get things done and is smart enough to do it for them. This is how Copilot works with some well-known Microsoft programs:

Copilot in Word

Copilot in Word alters the way you write swiftly and creatively. You can use it to produce, summarize, comprehend, improve, and enhance your writing. You can now use improved functionality, such as seeing and turning text into a table, adding to existing questions, making a document by referring to up to three documents and obtaining information about your document.

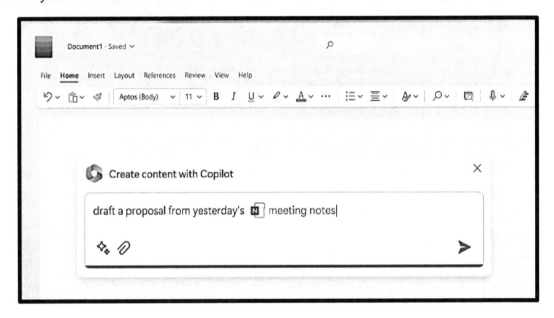

Copilot makes it simple to produce a first draft by suggesting ideas and expanding on what you've previously written. You may easily create tables from the text using Copilot's editing tools. Start a conversation with Copilot to learn more and enhance your work. If you are short on time, Copilot can summarize your document for you.

Copilot in Excel

In Excel, Copilot assists you in viewing and evaluating your data. When asking Copilot questions regarding your information, use real words rather than algorithms. Your inquiries will prompt it to make connections, generate what-if situations, and suggest new formulas. These models allow you to study your data without modifying it. To get diverse outcomes, look for trends, create striking images, or seek help.

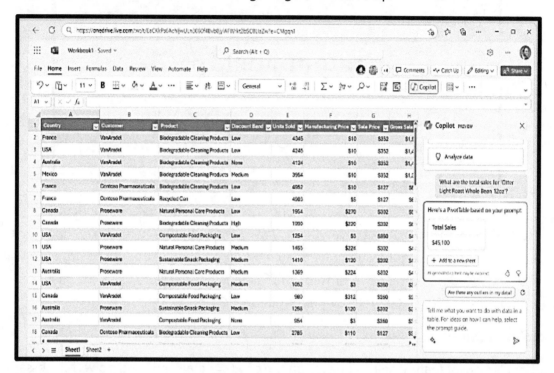

Copilot can help you better examine and comprehend your data. Find the most significant results quickly and view your data in an understandable format. You may easily highlight, filter, and organize your data to focus on what is important. Copilot's concepts for complex math make it easy to create formulas.

Copilot in PowerPoint

Copilot in PowerPoint makes it easier to create visually appealing slideshow presentations. Copilot can convert your existing written papers into decks complete with speaker notes and sources. It can also help you begin a fresh presentation with a basic prompt or idea.

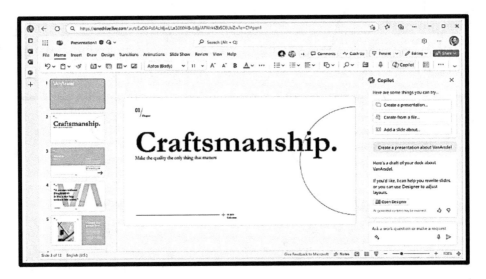

You can tell Copilot what to write about, and it will generate a preliminary copy of your presentation. Copilot features everything you need, whether you're creating a new presentation or need a quick summary of an existing one. Allow Copilot to organize your slides and quickly rearrange them to your liking. Furthermore, Copilot may create presentations or photos tailored to your organization's logo.

Copilot in Outlook

Outlook's Copilot feature helps you stay on top of your email and send powerful messages in much less time.

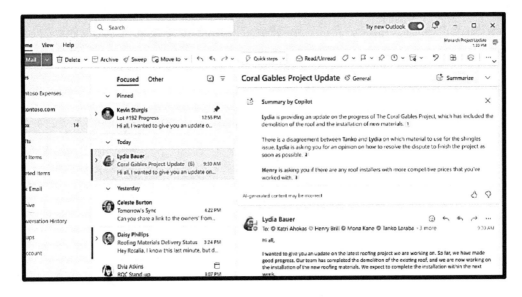

Copilot allows you to condense lengthy email conversations into brief summaries. You may now ask Copilot to summarize an email thread so you can quickly return to the original message and gain ideas for responses, action items, and follow-up meetings. When you write an email, you can also choose the length and tone.

Copilot in Teams

This feature in Teams called "Copilot" lets you easily summarize talks, carefully organize important points of discussion, and make meeting plans based on chat history.

During a meeting, you can summarize key themes from the discussion and make suggestions for what should be done. Get answers to specific inquiries and catch up on any material you may have missed to stay current. This ingenious application also simplifies the process of finding people to follow up with and scheduling follow-up meetings. This enhances your team's communication and leads to more work being completed.

Copilot in Viva

The cutting-edge AI tool in Microsoft Viva is called Copilot. It gives you quick, accurate, and customized answers and insights that are relevant to your business.

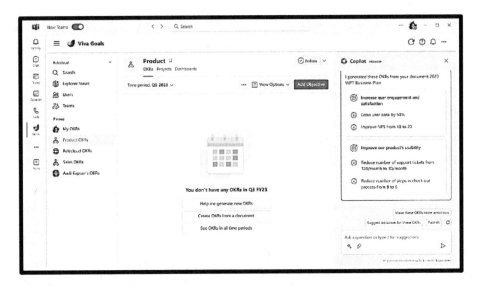

Conversational AI for Viva Goals Copilot makes it simple to establish and improve goals. Microsoft Viva Copilot uses next-generation AI to accelerate worker insights and increase staff engagement. It provides managers with predictive tools to help them construct a more connected and productive workforce. Copilot safeguards privacy, security, and compliance while promoting responsible AI usage and increased employee involvement.

Copilot in OneNote

OneNote's Copilot feature can help you change and organize your plan, so you can stay more organized and take action from your notes.

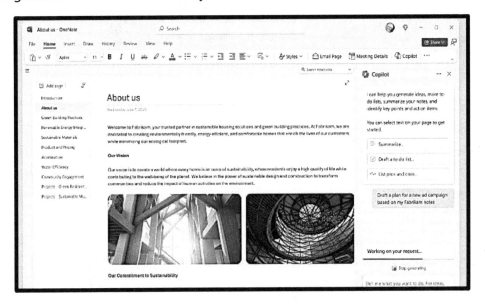

Allow Copilot to take your notes and transform them into actionable to-do lists. You can now get more out of your notes by asking more detailed questions, summarizing your content, or having Copilot create content for you. It may also help you write more clearly.

Copilot in Loop

Copilot in Loop lets you use the power of shared thought to co-create, catch up, and stay on the same page with your team.

Use Copilot's ideas to achieve your goals in Microsoft Loop. You may now use Copilot as a collaborative tool to make modifications. You can construct prompts and tables to assist manage team projects, take up where your teammates left off, summarize page information, and prepare a recap for a partner you're delegating work to.

Copilot in Whiteboard

Copilot in Whiteboard helps you get your brainstorming process going and speed it up so you can come up with, sort, and describe your ideas faster.

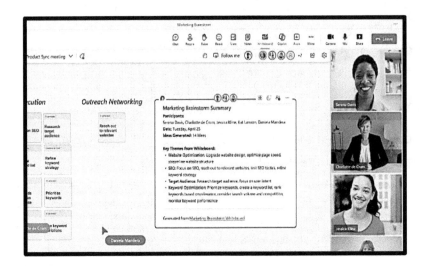

Copilot can describe complicated whiteboards, which makes it easy to share notes with Microsoft Loop. Work with other people, get feedback from Copilot on what you're making, and turn your brainstorming session into a finished show.

Microsoft Copilot in Team Communication

Microsoft Copilot is a key part of changing how teams talk to each other, making exchanges more streamlined to improve teamwork and productivity.

Facilitating Effective Communication

With its advanced AI features, Microsoft Copilot improves team communication by cutting down on mistakes and making things clearer.

- **Automated Meeting Summaries**: After a team meeting, Copilot can produce brief summaries that highlight the major points, decisions taken, and tasks to be completed. This keeps everyone in sync, even if they are unable to attend the meeting.
- **Action Item Tracking:** The copilot keeps track of action items from communications and meetings, giving notes to those responsible to make sure they follow through and making the team more accountable.
- **Real-time Language Translation**: Copilot's real-time translation removes language barriers, making it simple for people from different nations to collaborate. For example, a team from Germany, Japan, and the United States could work together on a project without any problems since Copilot would translate all messages in real-time, ensuring that everyone on the team understood all emails, meeting minutes, and project reports.

Automating Routine Communication Tasks

By automating routine conversations, Microsoft Copilot cuts down on the time needed for administrative tasks by a large amount.

- **Scheduling Meetings**: Copilot can simply locate times that are convenient for everyone on the team, taking into account their various time zones, and send out invitations. This saves time that would otherwise be spent back and forth setting up meetings.
- **Organizing Email Communications**: It can classify new emails by significance and compose responses to typical questions ahead of time, making email management easier and saving time.

This kind of technology has huge effects. One project team at a marketing firm said that after using Copilot, their routine costs went down by 30%. This gave them more time to work on strategic tasks like planning campaigns and keeping clients engaged.

Enhancing Team Dynamics and Productivity

Adding AI-powered communication tools like Microsoft Copilot changes the way teams work together and how much they get done.

- **Increased Transparency**: Automated reports and tracking make sure that everyone on the team has access to the same data, which builds trust and openness.
- **Faster Decision-Making**: Teams can make better decisions more quickly with the help of AI-driven insights and data analysis, which cuts down on project timelines.
- **More Inclusive Participation**: Tools like real-time translation and meeting reports make sure that everyone on the team can fully participate in team processes, no matter where they live or how well they speak the language.

A software development company that uses Microsoft Copilot as part of its workflow is an intriguing case study. The company's project completion times decreased significantly, and team morale increased dramatically. The team was able to focus on development because they could swiftly send out project updates and action items and had fewer administrative tasks to complete. This resulted in a 40% improvement in overall production.

Boosting Project Management with Microsoft Copilot

Microsoft Copilot is changing the way projects are managed by adding AI-powered accuracy and speed to old ways of doing things.

Streamlining Project Management

Microsoft Copilot changes the way projects are managed by making the planning and performance steps easier and better.

- **Data Analysis and Optimization**: This part looks at project data to predict possible delays and suggest ways to speed up work processes so that projects go easily and don't run into any problems that aren't necessary.
- **Predicting Bottlenecks**: Copilot lets you make changes ahead of time to keep things moving along and on schedule by predicting bottlenecks before they happen.

One significant application is for managing complex software development jobs. Copilot looks at previous data to uncover frequent problems in the development process and suggests changes ahead of time, such as moving resources around or adjusting deadlines, making project performance smoother.

Task Delegation and Progress Tracking

Microsoft Copilot shines when it comes to intelligently delegating tasks and keeping an eye on how projects are going in real-time.

- **Intelligent Task Delegation**: Copilot gives tasks to team members by looking at their skills, experience, and present workload. This makes sure that everyone is responsible for the right amount of work.
- **Real-time Progress Monitoring**: It keeps a close eye on project timelines and resource sharing, giving real-time reports on progress and pointing out areas that need more work.

Copilot was used by an engineering company to oversee a big building project. By using Copilot's features for delegating tasks and keeping track of progress, the company was able to cut the time it took to finish a project by 20% and make all team members happier by distributing work more fairly.

Case Studies in Project Management

Real-life examples of how Microsoft Copilot has changed the way projects are managed and how well they get done show how powerful it is.

- **Time Savings and Cost Reduction**: As a result, a global marketing firm cut costs and saved time by adding Copilot to its project management system. Project finish times were cut by 25%, and routine costs were cut by 15%, thanks to better job allocation and resource use.
- **Enhanced Team Coordination**: A technology company reported that adopting Copilot improved team communication and project results significantly. The platform's predictive analytics and real-time data aided the team in navigating a complex product launch with many moving components. As a result, the release was successful, on time, and exceeded stakeholders' expectations.

Microsoft Copilot for Collaborative Creativity and Problem-Solving

Teams can use Microsoft Copilot to work together and solve problems in new and creative ways.

- **Facilitating Creative Brainstorming:**

Discuss how Copilot may help individuals generate ideas, creative solutions, and data-driven insights during discussion gatherings. Emphasize that it can provide many points of view and generate false thinking circumstances to foster creativity.

- **Leveraging AI for Problem-Solving:**

Investigate how Copilot's AI-powered research can assist teams in identifying problems, generating potential solutions, and predicting what will happen. Demonstrate Copilot's ability to analyze massive volumes of data and generate solutions to difficult challenges.

- **Fostering a Collaborative Environment:**

Give examples of how to use Microsoft Copilot to promote teamwork and effective communication. Advice on how to utilize Copilot in a way that enhances teamwork rather than replacing it.

Integrating Microsoft Copilot into Existing Workflow Tools

Adding Microsoft Copilot to your existing collaborative and workflow solutions can help things operate more smoothly and efficiently. The effectiveness of this connection is critical for getting the most out of Copilot while not disrupting existing procedures.

Best Practices for Integration

Seamless Integration with Collaboration Platforms: If you want to combine Microsoft Copilot with Microsoft Teams, Asana, or Slack, you need to plan so that Copilot works with the other platform instead of on top of it.

- **Enhance, Don't Duplicate:** Make sure that Copilot's features add value to other tools without copying features. Instead, focus on areas that need to be automated or improved.
- **Customize Interactions:** Change the settings for Copilot to fit the way you communicate and handle projects on each platform, whether you're using Asana for official reports or Slack for more casual updates.

Integrating Copilot with Microsoft Teams demonstrates how to automate meeting scheduling and minutes. This saves project managers' time and increases team productivity.

Tailoring Copilot Functionality

By changing how Copilot works, you can make it fit your team's specific process needs.

- **Automating Routine Updates**: Set up Copilot to handle regular progress reports in project management software. This will allow team members to focus on more vital responsibilities.
- **Facilitating Data Collection**: You can set up Copilot to collect and combine data from different sources, so you don't have to manually put together reports.

One method Copilot was modified to match the routine of a development team was to automate sprint retrospectives. Copilot solicited feedback from individuals via Slack, compiled it, and presented it in a systematic format during sprint review meetings. This greatly improved the review process.

Ensuring Seamless Integration

Making it easy for Copilot to fit into current processes is important for both its usefulness and its popularity among users.

- **Phased Rollouts**: Put Copilot into use gradually so that teams may get used to the new features without feeling overwhelmed.
- **Continuous Feedback Loops**: Set up ways for users to provide feedback on how well Copilot functions and integrates with other apps. This will help the app continue to get better.
- **Training and Support**: Ensure that everyone on the team is comfortable and knowledgeable with Copilot's capabilities and knows how to use them with other tools by providing them with adequate training.

To ensure successful integration, focus on user acceptance through simplicity of use and demonstrate clear benefits. For example, a marketing business integrated Copilot into its content creation process. During focused training meetings, the team learned how to use Copilot inside their present Trello workflow. This improved the content approval procedure and helped them conclude the project on schedule.

Basic Commands and Functions

Microsoft Copilot integrates seamlessly with Visual Studio Code (VS Code) because it is a built-in application. Copilot does not have typical "commands" or "functions" as stand-alone software, but it does have numerous features and functions that may be accessed by keyboard shortcuts, code interactions, and concepts that are based on the present circumstances.

Some simple things you can do with Microsoft Copilot are listed below:

1. **Code Completion:** As you input code in VS Code, Copilot provides intelligent suggestions for how to complete the line based on what you're typing. To accept an idea, hit Tab or Enter, or use the arrow keys to navigate the options.

2. **Generating Code Snippets:** Copilot can generate complete code snippets from coder notes or natural language descriptions. To create a code snippet, simply provide a brief description of what you want to do in plain text or as a comment, and Copilot will make suggestions based on what you type.

3. **Keyboard Shortcuts:** You can use keyboard shortcuts to call up Copilot and start certain tasks or conversations. Even though Copilot doesn't have instructions, you can use the VS Code interface and keyboard shortcuts to get to its functions. For instance, you can use Ctrl+Space or Cmd+Space to bring up Copilot ideas.

4. **Contextual Assistance:** Copilot provides contextual guidance based on variable names, function labels, and surrounding code snippets. It examines the code's style and structure to provide you with suggestions and completions that make sense in this specific scenario.

5. **Learning and Adaptation:** Copilot is always learning and adapting based on how people interact with it and what they say. When you use Copilot and add its ideas to your code, it learns from these interactions and develops its models in order to provide better suggestions in the future.

6. **Feedback and Reporting:** If Copilot makes mistakes or suggests bad ideas, you can tell it so it can improve. You can leave comments directly in VS Code or via the feedback methods on GitHub.

7. **Privacy and Security Controls:** Copilot protects your privacy, and you can look at and change its privacy and security options as required. In your local work environment, you can control who can use Copilot and make sure that your data is treated safely.

Copilot lacks any self-executing instructions or functions, but it does have a plethora of tools and choices designed to improve coding in VS Code. With its intelligent code completion, code creation, and contextual support, developers can create code faster and better.

Mastering the User Interface and Navigation

We made the Copilot interface to be simple and easy to use, and it works with all of your other Microsoft 365 apps without any problems.

You can use the following steps to get to the Copilot tools in different M365 apps:

Word, Excel, and PowerPoint: You can get to Copilot in Word, Excel, and PowerPoint through the command bar and window. This is where you can make requests, see ideas, and make changes directly to your document, spreadsheet, or presentation.

Outlook: You can turn on Copilot in the email writing window to help you come up with content based on the email's context or the recipient's details.

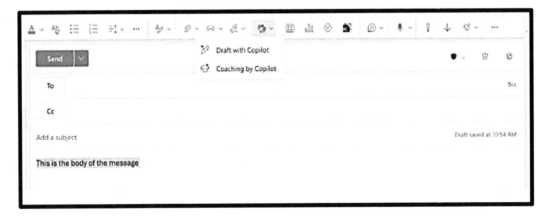

Teams: Team members can use the Copilot features to get help and work together in real-time during meetings or chats.

OneNote, Loop, and Whiteboard, Forms: Copilot is built into writing and creation tools like OneNote, Loop, Whiteboard, and Forms. It gives you ideas and help as you work on your projects.

When you first start using Copilot, it's helpful to get used to a few simple tasks and features:

- **Ask questions:** Type a question or request in normal words, and Copilot will answer or do something. Like "Summarize the most important parts of this document" in Word.
- **Create drafts:** Give Copilot a short description of what you need and ask it to write emails, papers, or slideshows.

- **Summarize content:** Copilot can quickly highlight the most important parts of long emails, papers, or slideshows when summarizing content.

Generating Code with Copilot

Using Copilot in Visual Studio Code, you can add AI-generated code to assist you write code by allowing you to chat in natural language. Power Pages allows you to edit aspects of a site using HTML, JS, or CSS code, which is not currently feasible in the Power Pages low-code design workshop.

This Copilot chat experience assists Power Pages developers like you in writing code by utilizing everyday language to express how you want the code to work. The code generated can then be improved and utilized to make modifications to your website. When you create code with Microsoft Copilot, it uses its AI-powered capabilities to provide you with clever code ideas and snippets based on notes or descriptions written in natural language.

In Visual Studio Code, here's how to use Copilot to write code:

1. **Install Copilot Extension:** Make sure the GitHub Copilot addon is installed in Visual Studio Code. If you search for "**GitHub Copilot**" on the Visual Studio Code Marketplace, you can locate and install it.

2. **Sign in to GitHub:** To access Copilot's features, log in to your GitHub account through Visual Studio Code. You can either click on the GitHub button in the sidebar or use Ctrl+Shift+P to open the command panel and perform the "GitHub: Sign In" command.

3. **Activate Copilot:** Copilot should be on by default once you're logged in. You can start using the tools of Copilot while writing code in Visual Studio Code.

4. **Generate Code Snippets:** You can provide Copilot with high-level details or comments about the functionality you want to add in order to generate code snippets. For example, if you wish to create a method that computes the factorial of a number, you may make a comment like this: # Calculate the factorial of a number. Copilot will read your response and generate code snippets to accomplish the task you specified. To use the produced code, all you have to do is accept Copilot's offer.

5. **Provide Context:** Copilot can only generate code snippets if your code and notes provide some context. When discussing the things you need, be as explicit and detailed as possible. The more information you provide, the more accurate and relevant the code snippets generated will be.

6. **Review and Modify Suggestions:** Once Copilot makes code suggestions, you should look them over to make sure they meet your needs and follow coding standards. You might need to change or adapt the code snippets that are created to fit your needs or the way you normally write code.

7. **Incorporate Generated Code:** It's possible to add created code to your codebase once you're happy with the code snippets that were produced. Copilot's ideas are made to work with your current code, so it's easy to add AI-generated features to your projects and make them better.

8. **Provide Feedback:** If Copilot generates incorrect or suboptimal code suggestions, you can provide input to help it improve. You can provide comments directly in Visual Studio Code or using the feedback options on GitHub.

By doing these things, you can use the AI-powered features of Microsoft Copilot to make code snippets quickly and easily in Visual Studio Code. This will help you be more productive as a coder.

Code Completion and Suggestions

Copilot excels at completing code in real-time. As you type, it gives intelligent suggestions based on the computer language and framework you have selected. This program not only allows you to code faster, but it also ensures that your work is proper. Some of the most essential features of Microsoft Copilot include code completion and suggestions, which are supposed to help developers create code more quickly.

Let me show you how code completion and ideas work in Copilot:

1. **Contextual Suggestions:** As you input code in Visual Studio Code (VS Code), Copilot suggests ideas that are related to what you're typing. The programming language, libraries, frameworks, and code snippets you use, as well as the suggestions, are all taken into consideration.

2. **Variable Names and Function Calls:** As you type, Copilot provides variable names, function names, method calls, and other code elements to help you

complete tasks quickly and correctly. These ideas are derived from best practices and general trends discovered in the data that Copilot's AI model learned from.

3. **Method Signatures and Parameters:** When you call functions or methods, Copilot will offer method signatures and parameter lists, which may contain input names and default values. This allows you to rapidly add the appropriate parameters to method or function calls.

4. **Error Correction and Validation:** Copilot can assist you in finding and correcting errors in your code by displaying various portions of code or highlighting grammar errors. It may also verify your code against common coding conventions and practices and give you ideas on how to improve or make it more efficient.

5. **Code Snippets and Templates:** Copilot offers brief pieces of code and templates for typical computing jobs and patterns. You can use these snippets to quickly create code without starting from scratch. They can range from basic sentences to full functions or classes.

6. **Natural Language Descriptions:** Copilot can obtain code snippets based on natural language descriptions or notes provided by the developer, in addition to traditional code completion. You can use simple English to describe the features you require, and Copilot will figure out what you mean and offer code to make those features work.

7. **Learning and Adaptation:** Copilot is always learning and adapting based on how people interact with it and what they say. When you use Copilot and add its ideas to your code, it learns from these interactions and develops its models in order to provide better suggestions in the future.

8. **Integration with Development Workflow:** Copilot works with VS Code's development process without any problems, giving ideas and completions right in the code editor. It's easy to add Copilot's ideas to your code because you can accept them with a single click.

Overall, Microsoft Copilot's code completion and ideas are meant to improve the coding experience by giving developers smart, context-aware help that lets them write code more quickly and correctly.

Contextual Understanding

Copilot leverages Microsoft Graphs to learn more about a person's context, including historical contacts and organizational data. This contextual knowledge ensures that the created material is helpful and relevant to the user's needs. Contextual knowledge is a crucial aspect of how Microsoft Copilot works. It refers to Copilot's ability to comprehend the situation in which code is produced and provide clever suggestions and completions that are suited for that situation.

In Microsoft Copilot, this is how contextual understanding works:

1. **Code Context Analysis:** As you input into your code editor (such as Visual Studio Code), Copilot monitors the coding environment in real-time. To determine what's going on in the code, it looks at things like variable names, function labels, notes, and other code snippets nearby.

2. **Syntax and Semantics:** Copilot examines the code and determines its meaning based on syntax and semantics. It identifies patterns, relationships, and dependencies in the code to provide you with accurate concepts and completions that adhere to the syntax and meaning of the computer language.

3. **Language and Library Awareness:** Copilot understands the computer language you're using and the libraries or tools in your project. It leverages this information to provide language-specific notions and completions, such as function names, method signatures, and APIs unique to a library.

4. **Code Patterns and Best Practices:** Copilot learns from a huge set of code from many places, such as GitHub's open-source libraries. From this information, it learns common coding patterns, idioms, and best practices, which it then uses to make ideas and complete sentences that make sense.

5. **Natural Language Interaction:** Copilot can read natural language comments or descriptions from developers while also understanding the code's context. You can use plain English to explain the functionality you require, and Copilot will create code snippets that fit your description while also taking into account the other codes around them.

6. **Real-time Feedback:** Copilot knows that context changes depending on how users engage with it and what feedback it receives. Copilot learns from your behaviors and improves its models to offer better recommendations in the future.

It accomplishes this by allowing you to accept or reject its ideas and incorporate them into your code.

7. **Accuracy and Relevance:** Copilot's contextual understanding is intended to provide correct and valuable ideas and completions, allowing developers to create code more quickly and correctly. Copilot's purpose is to deliver creative aid that suits the developer's needs and goals, looking at the context of the code being produced.

Overall, knowing the context is a key part of Microsoft Copilot's AI-powered features. This lets it offer smart code ideas and completions that are tailored to the current coding situation, language, and libraries being used.

CHAPTER 4

ADVANCED FEATURES OF MICROSOFT COPILOT

Microsoft Copilot has more advanced tools than just the ability to complete code and make suggestions. With these tools, developers can get more help and get more done with artificial intelligence.

The following are some of Microsoft Copilot's more powerful features:

1. **Code Generation from Comments:** Copilot can generate code based on the coder's comments or natural language assertions. Developers can direct Copilot to write the required code by writing a note that defines the desired feature in plain English.

2. **Refactoring Suggestions:** Copilot can make ideas for rewriting code, such as making it faster, easier to read, or more in line with best practices. It can find places in code that can be refactored and offer ways to make things better.

3. **Error Detection and Correction:** Copilot can assist you in finding and correcting errors in your code by recommending different lines of code or pointing out grammar errors. It can examine the code's context to identify potential issues and provide advice on how to resolve them.

4. **Complex Code Completion:** Copilot can handle complex coding circumstances and provide clever code completions for sophisticated language features such as functional programming, asynchronous programming, generics, and others.

5. **Integration with Git Version Control:** Copilot seamlessly integrates with Git version management, allowing developers to communicate with their Git files via Visual Studio Code. This integration allows you to commit changes, push and pull code, resolve merge issues, and view the history of commits.

6. **Enhanced Code Understanding:** Copilot is always learning from how people engage with it and what they say, allowing it to better comprehend code context, linguistic meanings, and programming trends. Over time, it may shift to other ways of creating code, managing projects, and collaborating with developers.

7. **Customization and Configuration:** Copilot lets you change how it works to fit your needs and the needs of your project. To get the most out of Copilot, developers can change settings for code ideas, privacy, security, and more.

8. **Cross-Language Support:** Copilot works with a variety of computer languages and can generate clever concepts as well as entire code in several languages and frameworks. It can seamlessly switch between languages in a project and provide language-specific assistance as needed.

9. **Code Snippet Expansion:** Depending on the information provided, Copilot can convert code snippets into completely functional apps. This tool allows developers to easily add templates, boilerplate code, or common patterns without having to write them manually.

10. **Feedback Mechanisms:** Copilot welcomes user feedback in order to improve its accuracy and functionality. Developers can report problems, offer modifications, or make general remarks through the feedback channels in Visual Studio Code and GitHub.

All of these advanced features make developers more productive and improve their coding experience by giving them smart help, automation, and insights throughout the development process.

Exploring Extensively Large Language

AI is transforming the world, and large language models (LLMs) are at the heart of it, particularly in apps such as Copilot for Microsoft 365. These models are distinguished by their ability to read and write language that appears to have been written by a human. In LLMs, the term "large" indicates two different things. Before everything else, it pertains to the models' sizes, which take into account a variety of criteria. Second, it alludes to the massive volumes of data that these models are trained on.

LLMs are more capable of understanding language subtleties and intricacies than AI models that are merely broad. LLMs are what enable Copilot for Microsoft 365 to work. They enable the creation of several features that alter how people interact with technology. These LLMs, which are hosted on Microsoft's Azure OpenAI Service, allow Copilot to process and respond to user inputs in a way that is similar to chatting with a human.

To accomplish this, you must first grasp the specifics of what consumers are asking for and then devise responses that are appropriate for each scenario. One of the most essential things Copilot does is leverage these LLMs to improve the work experience for its users.

By connecting to various Microsoft 365 apps, Copilot can give smart, situational suggestions and tips that boost efficiency and productivity.

Copilot's use of LLMs ensures that help is constantly available, automatically recognizing and answering users' needs, whether they are writing an email in Outlook, creating a document in Word, or preparing for a presentation in PowerPoint.

When using LLMs in Copilot, great care is taken to preserve privacy and data security. Microsoft ensures that, while Copilot employs LLMs to improve its functionality, it also adheres to all privacy and data protection requirements. This balance is critical for maintaining user trust, particularly given the importance of data security.

To summarize, Large Language Models perform multiple functions in Copilot for Microsoft 365. They enable Copilot to interpret and write content that appears to have been authored by a human, as well as to make user engagement simple, rapid, and safe. Adding LLMs to Copilot is a significant step in developing AI apps that are smarter and more valuable for humans.

What is the Large Language Model's Role in Copilot for Microsoft 365?

- **The core of Language Capabilities:** LLMs take user input and write human-like writing that makes sense in the given situation.
- **Understanding and Response Generation:** They figure out what the user is asking and write the right answers.
- **Foundation for AI Interactions:** LLMs are a key part of Copilot's smart interaction with Microsoft 365 apps.
- **Enhancing User Experience:** Their advanced language processing makes users much more efficient and productive.

Natural Language Processing (NLP) in Copilot for Microsoft 365

NLP: Bridging Human and Machine Language

Natural language processing (NLP) is a critical component of Copilot for Microsoft 365. It connects human language to machine understanding. NLP enables Copilot to read and understand writing in the same way that a human would, resulting in natural and logical answers. This technology is critical for translating complex human language into a format that computers can understand and process. This ensures that transactions with Copilot are fluid and rapid.

Key NLP Components

- **Tokenization:** This procedure divides text into smaller units, such as words or sentences. This simplicity is vital for AI to grasp, and it facilitates Copilot's reading and processing of information. Breaking words down into tokens allows Copilot to better comprehend the structure and meaning of what users are typing, resulting in more accurate answers.
- **Semantic Analysis:** To understand language, you must first understand what it signifies and how it fits into the larger context. Copilot can read more than just the words in a text since semantic analysis allows it to grasp what the text means. This understanding is essential for Copilot to assist you in all of your Microsoft 365 apps in a meaningful and informed manner.
- **Sentiment Analysis:** Copilot uses sentiment analysis to figure out how someone feels about something written down.

This analysis helps us understand what the person was seeking to improve. For example, Copilot can alter the tone and content of its response according to whether the user's request is urgent or not. This makes the contact more personal and useful.

- **Language Translation:** Copilot can assist people who speak different languages by utilizing NLP to communicate between them. In today's globalized labor market, this capability is especially useful. It enables Copilot to overcome language barriers and facilitates cross-lingual communication in Microsoft 365 apps.

Models Incorporating Copilot with Microsoft Graph

Microsoft Graph is the structure that connects all of the Microsoft 365 services and data. It's what makes Copilot for Microsoft 365 work, and it lets it find and combine information from many sources in a user's tenant.

- **Unifying Data Sources:** Graph brings together data from services like Outlook, OneDrive, SharePoint, Teams, and more, creating a single pool of data that Copilot can use.
- **Context-Rich Information:** By combining data from these different sources, Copilot can get a lot of context, which makes its answers more relevant and correct.

Contextual and Secure Data Access

Microsoft Graph not only combines data, but it also makes sure that the data that Copilot for Microsoft 365 can access meets the strictest security and safety standards.

- **Compliance and Security:** When Copilot talks to Microsoft Graph, it follows strict security measures and compliance rules. This makes sure that answers are based on information the user can see.
- **Role-Based Access Controls:** The Microsoft Graph API is very important for keeping role-based access controls up to date. This makes sure that the answers from Copilot for Microsoft 365 are safe and follow company rules.

Using the benefits of Microsoft Graph, Copilot for Microsoft 365 can provide a seamless, secure, and tightly integrated user experience across all Microsoft 365 apps. Adding this option makes Copilot more useful and efficient, and it ensures that user data is handled carefully and in accordance with company and government regulations.

Utilizing Copilot for Sophisticated Data Analysis

It is the copilot's job to help the pilot navigate the plane, follow procedures, carry out orders, and give the captain corrects information right away so that the captain can make choices that are safe for the flight. Think about the role of First Officer Jeff Skiles played by Aaron Eckhart in the movie "Sully."

When their plane has problems, he jumps into action right away to help Captain Sullenberger by giving him data, running checklists, checking different states, and helping the captain make an important choice in any way he can.

Real-life boardrooms aren't too far behind when it comes to having to act quickly under a lot of stress. Business leaders also need a copilot to help them handle high-stakes scenarios, handle crises right away, spot possible red flags ahead of time, and work quickly.

Copilots for Data Analytics meet this need and make sure that business leaders can make decisions and do their daily work without any problems.

What is a copilot for data analytics? How do copilots impact data analytics?

A copilot for Data Analytics is an artificial intelligence (AI) assistant that assists users in automating time-consuming manual tasks, communicating with enterprise data in simple terms, identifying actionable insights and presenting them in understandable narratives, and personalizing the information experience.

Generative AI, Natural Language Processing (NLP), Machine Learning (ML), and Large Language Models (LLMs) are powerful technologies used by the AI copilot to generate and share ideas. A data analytics copilot is a skilled data analyst, a personal business assistant, a reliable guide, the primary person who makes things happen, and an engaging assistant.

It has been a long time since data analytics was limited to technical researchers. Now, non-technical business users are encouraged to perform analytics. Copilots make data analytics even easier by making data easier to access, data queries easier to interpret, and insights easier to apply and implement.

Users can ask queries like, "Why did demand for Product ABC rise in Q1?" and receive immediate responses in the form of text descriptions and best-fit photos. AI copilots are increasingly being deployed in non-data analytics sectors. For example, GitHub Copilot, Amazon CodeWhisperer, and Microsoft Copilot have all been proved to be effective for developing and reviewing code, writing code and ideas, and creating texts and content assets to assist users in being more productive and making fewer mistakes.

GitHub discovered that developers who used GitHub copilot were 30% more productive. Copilots have been utilized in various sectors to speed up the completion of work, save mental energy that would have been spent on repeated tasks, and make workers happier and more focused at work.

Maximizing data analytics efficiency by leveraging the copilot's dynamic features

A data analytics copilot accelerates the process of extracting meaningful information from unstructured data, from data preparation to insight generation. This simplifies the work of data engineers and researchers and allows business customers more control over their information requirements. Here are some of the ways that copilot's features help make data analytics more efficient:

Curate and enrich data automatically

Copilot may assist improve corporate data by adding synonyms, creating usable labels for data rows and columns, discovering links between them, and classifying and structuring data so that it can be studied effectively and properly.

Provide suggestions to improve quality.

The quality of thoughts is directly proportional to the quality of data. Copilots can report on the quality of data and give suggestions for how to improve it in terms of being full, clear, readable, consistent, and correct.

Ask questions in simple language.

Users do not have to deal with complex language or SQL searches to obtain information. Copilot enables customers to ask inquiries directly about their business data using natural language and simple tools. Copilots can also generate search suggestions based on company data, which simplifies the search process. This allows everyone in an organization to obtain data and insights.

Leverage LLMs to parse human language queries better

People's language is full of jargon, slang, unplanned phrases, non-standard spelling, and words that might mean different things in different contexts. Copilots employ the benefits of LLMs to interpret natural language inquiries, determine the proper context to provide helpful information and eliminate extraneous stuff.

Create narratives and audio-visual data stories.

Data analytics copilots may create insight stories, written summaries, audiovisual data stories, live presentations, and visually appealing visuals more quickly and easily. Users may readily grasp business circumstances, discuss and exhibit summarized findings in a better way, and feel confident in their judgments when they use these automatically generated content formats.

Provide tailored insights and business headlines.

Copilots can give appropriate suggestions and insights based on the user's previous searches, usage habits, interests, company analytics, and searches performed. They can also get rid of useless data. Business headlines can be programmed to generate and disseminate ideas without users needing to hunt for them.

Who can benefit from using Copilot for data analytics?

Many user roles in a company can use data analytics copilots to make their work more productive and efficient.

Data Engineers and Stewards

Copilots help data engineers and data stewards clean, organize, and get the business data ready. By simplifying manual, time-consuming, and repeating tasks, copilots can process data more quickly, find and fix problems more quickly, and free up the data teams to work on new ideas and more difficult tasks.

Data Scientists and Analysts

Copilots assist data scientists and analysts in discovering connections in massive volumes of data and better organizing it to make it more valuable, making business jargon easier to grasp, and giving data more meaning by developing automatic words, easy-to-remember names, and meaningful descriptions. Copilots assist analysts in ensuring that reliable data is always available for analysis by identifying problems with the quality of the data and recommending solutions.

Business Users

Business users such as product managers, sales representatives, financial officers, marketing leaders, and customer success agents can utilize copilots to ask natural data inquiries, gain real-time insights, and receive personalized recommendations. Copilot also allows corporate users to create dynamic panels and results on their own. Copilots help people comprehend insights faster and better by creating summaries of key outcomes, audiovisual data tales, and bite-sized insights.

Potential use cases for copilot in data analytics

Here are some ways that copilots can improve business processes across organizations, with AI-powered analytics giving them more information and helping them make better choices:

Sales

Sales managers may swiftly compare sales across various dimensions by asking natural language inquiries about periods, geographies, goods, and client groups. They can also determine which items have the largest profit margins, which products are the most popular, and any other sales fluctuations that are not logical. Getting immediate responses can help them keep a watch on sales, figure out where growth is lagging or speeding up, and move right away.

Banking

A data analytics copilot allows bankers to ask simple questions such as "loans disbursed in Q1", "what is the percentage of high net-worth customers", "compare deposits from 2018 to 204", and "By how much did savings deposits increase in the North West region", "most preferred banking products in 2024", and so on. In this manner, they don't have to go through transaction records, financial statements, and customer information. Copilots can also provide information about someone's creditworthiness, generate business ideas, and warn against activities that appear suspicious.

Retail

Retailers are constantly attempting to discover what their customers want, what motivates them to buy certain items, and how and why their preferences shift. Stores can easily answer all of these questions using data analytics copilots. Retailers can learn more about trends and better serve their consumers by asking copilots questions such as "What are the best stores in 2024?" and "Which discount coupons were used the most in December

2023?" This allows them to better understand the needs of their clients and improve their service.

Customer Support

Copilots can show you what kinds of requests people are making, what questions they are asking a lot, and what problems they are having most of the time. These tips can help people who work in customer service solve problems faster, give better advice, and make sure customers are happier. Product development teams can get useful information and ideas from customer support data to make goods, the customer journey, and the general experience better.

Marketing

Marketing teams must communicate with their customers in a way that generates results. When marketing professionals utilize copilot for data analytics, they can identify the most trafficked channels, compare the leads generated by various social media platforms, assess campaign success, and track their marketing budget and spending. By reading recaps of major results, they can better comprehend not only what happened, but also why and how. This offers them a complete picture.

Human Resource Management

Copilots can assist HR managers in determining what skills and training are required, the effectiveness of training, and employee performance. Simple queries, such as "Who are the best sales reps?" "What is the ratio of developers to testers in a project?" "What was the turnover rate in 2023?" "How many employees are proficient in Python?" and other similar questions can assist HR managers manage and enhance their teams.

Benefits of using copilot for data analytics

Artificial intelligence (AI)--powered copilots for data analytics help people process and analyze data to find insights. According to a poll of business owners by Forbes Advisor in 2023, AI is seen as a benefit because it helps people make better decisions (44%), respond faster (53%), and avoid mistakes (48%).

Faster insights

Copilots make data analysis easier and help users quickly find root causes, get useful insights in real-time, see everything going on in a business, and easily do complicated analyses.

Improved data-driven decision-making

Decision-makers can better spot trends, patterns, and differences when they have personalized, easy-to-understand insight reports. This teaches people how to make decisions based on facts.

Ease of use

Copilots make it easy for business users to connect with company data, even if they don't know much about technology. They do this by using a conversational and natural interface.

Accelerated data processing

Copilot allows customers to automate data cleaning and processing, improve data preparation procedures, increase efficiency, and reduce the time it takes to get good-quality data available for analysis.

Improved productivity

Copilots give users the tools they need to do self-service analytics, which lets them act quickly and work efficiently, saving a lot of time and resources in the process of finding insights.

Improved data literacy

Copilots for data analytics give users trust in their analysis by removing technological barriers and simplifying the insight search process. This increases analytics adoption, improves data literacy, and fosters a data-driven organizational culture.

Investigating Copilot's Complete Range of Capabilities

To fully understand what Microsoft Copilot can do, you need to look into all of its features, functions, and possible uses. Additionally, Copilot can do many other things besides just writing code. Its main job is to provide clever code ideas and completions.

Here is an outline of all the things that Copilot can do:

1. **Code Completion and Suggestions:** Copilot provides intelligent suggestions about how to finish writing code based on what is being written. It helps programmers create code more quickly by proposing names for variables, functions, method calls, and other portions of code.

2. **Code Generation from Comments:** Copilot can make code snippets based on developer notes or natural language explanations. Developers can tell Copilot to write the necessary code by leaving a note that describes the desired feature in plain English.

3. **Code Refactoring Suggestions:** Copilot gives you code rewriting ideas, like how to make code run faster, read better, or follow best practices. It can find places in code that can be refactored and offer ways to make things better.

4. **Error Detection and Correction:** Copilot can assist you in finding and correcting errors in your code by recommending different lines of code or pointing out grammar errors. It can examine the code's context to identify potential issues and provide advice on how to resolve them.

5. **Cross-Language Support:** Copilot works with a variety of computer languages and can generate clever concepts as well as entire code in several languages and frameworks. It can seamlessly switch between languages in a project and provide language-specific assistance as needed.

6. **Integration with Git Version Control:** Copilot seamlessly integrates with Git version management, allowing developers to communicate with their Git files via Visual Studio Code. This integration allows you to commit changes, push and pull code, resolve merge issues, and view the history of commits.

7. **Privacy and Security Controls:** Copilot protects your privacy, and developers can look at and change its privacy and security options as required. Copilot only stores and sends code fragments and user data within the local working environment. This protects the privacy and security of the data.

8. **Learning and Adaptation:** Copilot is always learning and adapting based on how people interact with it and what they say. When developers use Copilot and add ideas to their code, it learns from these interactions and develops its models in order to provide better suggestions in the future.

9. **Natural Language Interaction:** Copilot can do more than just write code. It also understands natural language comments or descriptions provided by the creator. Developers can describe the functionality they require in plain English, and Copilot will instantly generate code snippets that match what they say.

10. **Customization and Configuration:** Copilot lets you change how it works to fit your needs and the needs of your project. To get the most out of Copilot, developers can change settings for code ideas, privacy, security, and more.

By learning more about these features, developers can use Microsoft Copilot to get more done, write better code, and speed up the development process for a wide range of projects and tasks.

CHAPTER 5

USING COPILOT EFFECTIVELY

To get the most out of Microsoft Copilot, you need to use its features and functions to improve your writing and get more done.

Here are some useful tips for using Copilot:

1. **Understand Copilot's Capabilities:** Learn about Copilot's capabilities and functions, including code completion, generation, error detection, and natural language interaction. Learning about Copilot's capabilities will allow you to use it to its full potential.

2. **Provide Clear Context:** When you provide code or comments about functions, provide Copilot with clear and concise context so that it can comprehend what you mean. When the issue is obvious, the copilot can generate more accurate and helpful ideas.

3. **Review Suggestions Carefully:** Copilot makes smart suggestions, but you need to carefully read them over before adding them to your code. Make sure that the code snippets that were offered meet your needs, follow coding standards, and fit with the design of your project.

4. **Validate Generated Code:** If you use Copilot to generate code from natural language statements, ensure that the code you create works as intended. Using your coding environment, test the code elements and make any necessary adjustments.

5. **Provide Feedback:** Please notify Copilot if it provides you with incorrect or suboptimal suggestions so that it can improve its performance. You can provide comments directly in Visual Studio Code or using the feedback options on GitHub.

6. **Customize Settings:** You can modify Copilot's settings to make it perform as you want and match the requirements of your project. To get the most out of Copilot, adjust the settings for code ideas, privacy, security, and other things.

7. **Integrate with Git:** To accelerate your work, use Copilot's interface with Git version control. In Visual Studio Code, you can use Git commands to make changes, push and pull code, resolve merge issues, and view the history of contributions.

8. **Stay Informed:** To find out about changes and improvements to Copilot, keep an eye on what Microsoft and GitHub say. To get the newest features and improvements, make sure you regularly update your Visual Studio Code and Copilot application.

9. **Learn Keyboard Shortcuts:** To get more done when coding, study and apply the keyboard tools included with Copilot. Learn about the tools you can use to access Copilot's features, ask for ideas, and accept completions.

10. **Practice and Experiment:** To improve your Copilot skills, practice using it in various code settings and become acquainted with its features. The more you use Copilot, the better you'll grasp what it can accomplish and how to apply those abilities in your projects.

If you follow these tips, you'll be able to use Microsoft Copilot to improve the quality of your software projects, write code more quickly, and get more done.

Best Practices for Utilizing Copilot

To get the most out of Microsoft Copilot and keep the quality of your code high, you need to follow some best practices.

Here are some tips on how to use Copilot most effectively:

1. **Understand Copilot's Scope and Limitations:** Learn about what Copilot can and cannot accomplish. Even though Copilot can be useful, it's vital to note that it's not flawless and may not always give you the best advice.

2. **Provide Clear Context:** When using Copilot, provide clear context by using comments and code to clarify what you're doing. Copilot can better comprehend your aims and come up with better ideas if you articulate them simply and concisely.

3. **Review and Validate Suggestions:** Before incorporating Copilot's suggestions into your script, always read them thoroughly. Check the developed code to make sure it satisfies your needs, follows the standards for writing code, and fits your project's design.

4. **Be Selective with Suggestions:** Don't merely follow Copilot's ideas without considering what they mean. Consider factors such as readability, maintainability, and speed when deciding what concepts to incorporate into your code.

5. **Supervise Copilot's Output:** Copilot can make code snippets, but it's important to watch what it does and make any changes that are needed. Make sure that the code that is created works well with the code that you already have and doesn't add any mistakes or security holes.

6. **Use Copilot as a Learning Tool:** Do not utilize Copilot instead of learning to code. Instead, use it to enhance your learning. Copilot allows you to experiment with new ways of creating code, learn from its suggestions, and gain a deeper understanding of fundamental computer concepts.

7. **Provide Feedback:** If Copilot gives you wrong or less-than-ideal ideas, please let it know so it can get better at doing its job. Copilot's models and algorithms are always getting better thanks to your input.

8. **Balance Automation with Manual Coding:** Use Copilot's automation features while still writing code by hand. Some coding chores can be done faster with Copilot, but manual coding provides better control and precision, especially in crucial or challenging scenarios.

9. **Maintain Code Consistency:** Make sure that your codebase uses the same writing style, naming standards, and design patterns. To keep the code easy to read and manage, Copilot's ideas should match your project's coding standards and conventions.

10. **Stay Informed about Updates:** Follow Microsoft and GitHub releases to stay up to date on Copilot upgrades and enhancements. Update your Copilot app frequently to receive the most recent features and bug fixes.

By using these best practices, you can get the most out of Microsoft Copilot to improve the quality of your code, speed up development processes, and make your writing more productive.

Improving Productivity with Copilot

AI (artificial intelligence) has been a part of our online lives for a long time, making personalized news reports, friend ideas, email autocomplete hints, and other things. With Microsoft 365 Copilot, AI can now do everything it was meant to do. Copilot works with Word, Excel, PowerPoint, Outlook, Teams, and other popular Microsoft apps without any problems to give you real-time, personalized help.

The astonishing transition from "AI on autopilot" to "AI as copilot" Copilot provides secure, enterprise-level AI by merging the capabilities of large language models (LLMs) with your company data. This makes it one of the most effective productivity tools in the world. Copilot offers a new way of working to the table, allowing employees to boost their creativity, output, and abilities while spending less time on mundane activities. CoPilot 365 makes routine jobs more productive by using conventional apps.

Here are three ways to use Microsoft 365 copilot:

- **Automated Data Analysis in Excel:** CoPilot 365 can perform complex data analysis tasks in Excel automatically. For example, it can swiftly look at patterns, do sophisticated math, and produce extensive reports, saving hours of labor that would otherwise have to be done manually.
- **Efficient Email Management in Outlook:** It helps you deal with your emails by putting important ones at the front of the list, scheduling responses, and organizing your inbox so you spend less time sifting them.
- **Improved Document Creation in Word:** CoPilot 365 helps you create better papers by suggesting methods to improve the content, providing formatting options, and even creating text for you based on brief instructions. This makes the process of creating documents considerably faster.

Here are five ways that Copilot can help you get more done:

1. **Write, edit, and summarize text in Word**

To get the most out of Word, offer Copilot brief instructions on how to do tasks while you work. Copilot can create drafts of papers, summarize material, rework sections of documents, change their tone, and more.

Examples of commands:

- Make the document sound less formal.
- Reduce the length of the third paragraph.
- Use the information from [a document] and [a table] to write a two-page plan.

2. **Unlock insights, identify trends, and generate powerful data visualizations in Excel.**

Copilot in Excel allows you to rapidly glance over and evaluate your data. Copilot can help you make smart decisions and reach your goals by providing relevant information, clever ideas, and impressive visualizations.

Examples of commands:

- Show how the sales are broken down by type and channel. Put it on a table.
- Make a chart to help you see what the effects of changing [a variable] will be.
- Figure out what would happen to my profit margin if the growth rate for [variable] changed.

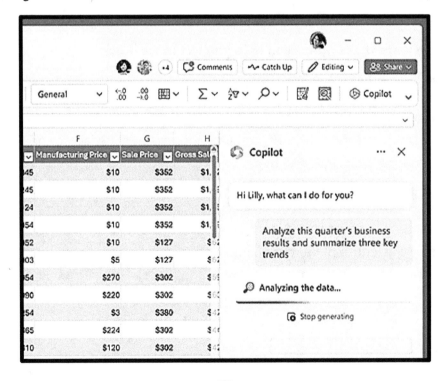

3. Accelerate the creation process and produce dynamic presentations in PowerPoint.

You can use Copilot in PowerPoint to create stunning slideshows, alter current slides, and add fascinating animations. Copilot can speed up your work and assist you in producing high-quality shows that make maximum use of all the features and tools available.

Examples of commands:

- Make a file slide show from [a paper] and add important stock photos.
- This talk should be summed up in three slides.
- Put these three bullet points in three boxes, and give each one a picture.

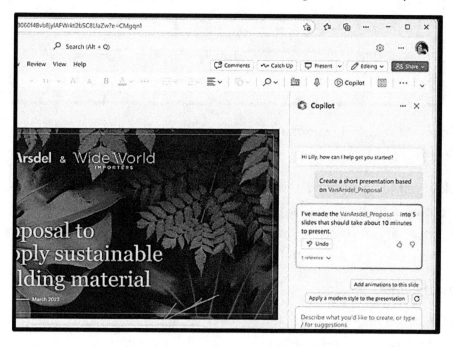

4. Manage your inbox and level up your communication in Outlook

Copilot eliminates the need to read through texts and take notes. Copilot in Outlook can organize emails, summarize long email lines, and create professional, high-quality notes. Copilot can include other emails or information from Microsoft 365 in your message.

Examples of commands:

- Write up a list of the emails I missed last week while I was away. Mark any important things.

- Write an answer thanking them and asking for more information about their second and third points. Cut this writing down and make it sound more professional.
- Next Thursday at noon, have a "lunch and learn" about new products with everyone. Say that food is given.

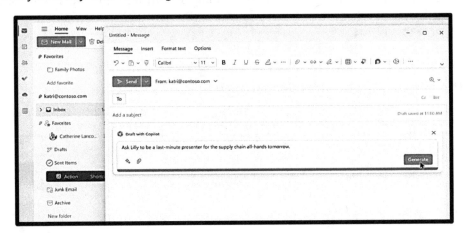

5. **Generate real-time summaries, create meeting agendas, and gain insights in Teams**.

Teams allow you to collaborate and communicate with Copilot more effectively. Copilot can use prompts to help you organize talking points, summarize essential activities, generate clever ideas, create agendas, and schedule follow-ups. This will make your meetings more effective and fruitful.

Examples of commands:

- Write down what I missed in the meeting. What have we talked about so far? Where do we differ about this subject?
- Make a list of the pros and cons of [the subject being talked about]. What else should we think about before we decide?
- What choices were made, and what do you think should happen next?

Using Microsoft Copilot's features and functions to simplify coding processes and improve coding efficiency is one way to boost productivity.

Here are some more ways that Copilot can help you be more productive:

1. **Accelerate Code Writing:** As you type, Copilot can propose and complete code for you. Copilot can help you autocomplete variable names, function calls, and code snippets so you don't have to enter them all by hand.

2. **Automate Repetitive Tasks:** Look for coding tasks or trends in your process that you do often and use Copilot to automate them. Based on what you describe, Copilot can make basic code, template structures, or common patterns. This saves you time and effort.

3. **Explore New Coding Patterns:** You can use Copilot to discover and test new code patterns, methods, and libraries. Try solving coding jobs in different ways, and follow Copilot's guidance to enhance your code knowledge and skills.

4. **Refactor Code Efficiently:** Copilot can assist with code rewriting by recommending approaches to improve readability, speed, and maintainability. Using Copilot's refactoring suggestions can help you speed up the process of optimizing and rearranging your code.

5. **Prototype Ideas Quickly:** When you're testing new features or concepts, Copilot can generate code scaffolds or sample versions based on your input. Rapid code creation via Copilot allows you to test and enhance ideas more quickly.

6. **Learn from Copilot's Suggestions:** While you're writing, pay attention to what Copilot says. Look at the code snippets and patterns that Copilot suggests to learn new phrases, best practices, and ways to code.

7. **Collaborate with Teammates:** Share Copilot's ideas and code snippets with your peers to facilitate collaboration and knowledge sharing. Copilot can assist your team follow the same coding guidelines and ensure that the quality of the code is always consistent.

8. **Optimize Documentation and Comments:** To make docs or comments for your script, use Copilot. Use normal language to explain how or why a piece of code works, and Copilot will create comments that go with it to make the code easier to read and manage.

9. **Stay Focused on High-Value Tasks:** Allow Copilot to handle the repetitive coding jobs so you may concentrate on more important activities such as architectural design, speed optimization, and feature addition. Allow Copilot to do the tedious,

repetitive writing labor while you focus on things that need you to think critically and creatively.

10. **Provide Feedback for Improvement:** Keep telling Microsoft and GitHub what you think of Copilot. Share your comments, ideas, and requests for new features to help Copilot become more accurate, helpful, and user-friendly over time.

These ideas will help you get the most out of Microsoft Copilot to make your software development projects more productive, your writing process more efficient, and the quality of your work higher.

Customizing Copilot Suggestions

By giving clear context, following coding standards, and changing the way you code, you can indirectly change the ideas.

Here are some good ways to change the ideas that Copilot makes:

1. **Clear Context:** To assist Copilot in comprehending your ideas better, ensure that the context in your code and notes is clear and concise. To assist Copilot make the appropriate choices, be very specific about the feature you're adding or the issue you're attempting to solve.

2. **Coding Style and Conventions:** Ensure that your project follows the same coding style and conventions throughout. Copilot learns from the patterns and styles in your files, thus ensuring that your code is consistent helps it generate ideas that are in accordance with the standards for your project.

3. **Feedback Mechanisms:** Tell Microsoft and GitHub what you think about Copilot's ideas, especially if you identify any that are incorrect or not very good. Your feedback enables Copilot to improve its models and algorithms, resulting in better ideas over time.

4. **Code Reviews:** Conduct regular code reviews with your team to go over Copilot's ideas. As part of the review process, discuss the quality and usefulness of the code snippets that Copilot developed, and make any necessary changes or fixes.

5. **Manual Intervention:** Even though Copilot generates ideas automatically, you remain in control of which code is added to your project. Carefully review Copilot's proposals and make any necessary adjustments or improvements manually to ensure the code matches your goals and standards.

6. **Experimentation and Learning:** Try out the ideas that Copilot gives you and learn from the code snippets that it creates. Check out the different coding patterns, methods, and ways that Copilot suggests to get better at writing code and understanding how programming works.

7. **Selective Acceptance:** Be selective about the Copilot ideas you include in your software. Check each idea to see if it aligns with your project's goals, is relevant, and can be read and maintained. You should only accept ideas that can improve your program and aid your project.

8. **Continuous Improvement:** Always search for ways to improve Copilot's ideas and your code. To gain better outcomes over time, provide Copilot feedback periodically, respond to changes in how it behaves, and enhance the way you code.

Even though Copilot doesn't have as many customization options as some other tools, these tips can help you change Copilot's ideas to better fit the goals and preferences of your project.

CHAPTER 6

WORKING WITH COPILOT IN DIFFERENT SCENARIOS

1. **Automated Data Analysis**: Every week, a financial specialist spends hours analyzing market patterns. With Copilot, they can enter data and receive a detailed report straight away, saving them hours of labor.

2. **Improved Efficiency in Excel**: An HR manager used to spend an entire day putting together measures for employee success. Copilot can complete this job in only a few hours, allowing you more time to prepare intelligently.

3. **AI-Powered Insights**: A marketing team uses Copilot to review consumer complaints. It immediately reveals the most relevant opinion patterns, enabling businesses to make better strategic choices.

4. **Error Reduction**: An accountant who writes data by hand makes a lot of mistakes. These mistakes are less likely to happen with Copilot's formula ideas and data checking, which makes financial reports more reliable.

5. **Quick Formula Generation**: When a researcher is looking at enormous amounts of complex data, Copilot can assist them locate important formulas. This speeds up the analysis process and reduces the time it takes to create formulas by hand.

6. **Time-Saving in Report Generation**: It used to take a project manager several hours to put together project progress reports, but now they use Copilot to quickly gather data and make full reports.

7. **Improved Decision-Making**: A sales manager examines sales figures from several areas using Copilot. The knowledge provided allows them to better employ their resources, which leads to greater sales.

8. **Easy Data Visualization**: A school teacher who wants to see how students are doing across several different factors now uses Copilot to make maps. This makes it easier to see quickly which areas need more work.

9. **Interactive Data Exploration**: A store business analyst uses Copilot to look into sales data and interact with it to find secret trends and useful information.

10. **Enabled Workflows**: A transportation assistant manages inventory data with Copilot. It makes their job easier and makes it easier to keep track of stock and replace it.

11. **Personalized Data Handling**: A sales executive can customize Copilot such that it only displays critical success indicators relevant to their aims. In this manner, customers can receive tailored reports that assist them plan their strategy.

12. **Collaboration Improvement**: Copilot lets members of a cross-functional team doing market research work together to study and make sense of data. This improves teamwork and understanding.

13. **Learning Curve Reduction**: A non-profit with little technical know-how utilizes Copilot to make sophisticated Excel capabilities easy to use, allowing workers to execute advanced data chores without having to go through a lot of training.

14. **Cost-Effectiveness**: A small business owner who doesn't have the money to buy expensive data analysis tools can process complex data with Copilot, which means they don't have to buy any more software.

15. **Real-Time Data Processing**: An operations manager uses Copilot to handle real-time inventory data, which lets them make decisions about transportation and restocking right away.

16. **Support for Complex Calculations**: An environmental scientist utilizes Copilot to perform complex statistical analyses that would normally require special statistical tools.

17. **Intuitive User Interface**: An independent writer who doesn't know much about Excel uses Copilot because it's easy to use and helps them organize and analyze research data quickly.

18. **Customizable Outputs**: A financial consulting company changes the outputs from Copilot to fit its reporting style. This makes it easier to make reports for clients.

19. **Data Integrity Maintenance**: An academic researcher uses Copilot to analyze data, ensuring that the security of their study data is maintained throughout the process.

20. **Flexible Data Manipulation**: In a transportation company, the supply chain manager utilizes Copilot to change package data in a number of ways, which helps find the optimal routes and reduces shipping costs.

21. **Improved Data Interpretation**: A real estate company uses Copilot to make sense of complicated market data, which lets managers give their clients better tips on how to invest in real estate.

22. **Productivity Tracking**: An IT company uses Copilot to monitor the development of a project. This makes it easy to determine how productive people are and how much work they need to complete.
23. **Scalable Solutions**: An e-commerce company that is growing uses Copilot's scalable features to handle more sales data without having to spend a lot of money on more IT staff.
24. **Secure Data Handling**: A healthcare provider trusts Copilot to keep patient data safe and secure in meeting privacy and security standards.
25. **Integration with Microsoft Suite**: The fact that Copilot works with Microsoft Suite makes it easier for a law company to prepare documents and analyze data across multiple programs.
26. **Reduced Training Requirements**: A public school system employs Copilot, which reduces instructors' requirement for rigorous Excel training, saving time and resources.
27. **Accessibility Features**: An NGO with staff members who aren't all tech-savvy uses Copilot and likes how its accessibility features make data analysis more open to everyone.
28. **Language Support**: Copilot's growing language support enables an international company's workforce to communicate and share data more readily around the world.
29. **Continuous Improvement**: The changes and improvements to Copilot help a tech company keep its data analysis tools on the cutting edge.
30. **Future-Proofing**: An investing company keeps up with technology by using Copilot to train its personnel for new AI developments and changes in the sector.

Software Development

To make Copilot work well for you in software development, follow these steps:

1. **Installation**: First, add the GitHub Copilot app to Visual Studio Code. You can find "GitHub Copilot" in VS Code's store of addons and install it that way.
2. **Enable Copilot**: To switch on Copilot, you may need to check in to your GitHub account after downloading. As soon as you turn on Copilot, it begins offering suggestions while you type code.

3. **Contextual Suggestions**: Copilot examines the background of your code and generates ideas based on its findings. The code you've already written can help it generate variable names, function names, code completions, and even full functions or blocks of code.

4. **Interactiveness**: You can speak with Copilot. As you type, it provides code completions. You can accept or reject these concepts by hitting the Tab key. You may also use the arrow keys to move between several concepts.

5. **Code Generation**: Copilot may use Python, JavaScript, TypeScript, Ruby, Go, Java, and other computer languages to create programs. It is very useful for repetitive tasks or creating basic programming.

6. **Learning and Feedback**: The code you write and the updates you make allow Copilot to learn. It becomes smarter over time and generates better ideas based on how you code and what you enjoy.

7. **Code Review Assistance**: Copilot can assist with code reviews by suggesting modifications that will improve the code or highlighting potential issues. This can assist ensure that code quality and accuracy are maintained throughout the whole project.

8. **Privacy and Security**: Take caution with the code you give Copilot, especially if it contains private information. Copilot does not keep your code, but it does learn from the code it sees. Be cautious utilizing Copilot with codebases that are private or owned by someone else.

9. **Feedback and Reporting**: If you use Copilot and run into any bugs or strange behavior, you can let GitHub know. Reporting problems and giving comments helps the tool get better over time.

10. **Continuous Learning**: Continue to investigate Copilot's capabilities and suggestions. Experiment with various types of writing to determine when and how it can most benefit your growth process.

By incorporating Copilot into your software development process, you can increase productivity, spend less time manually creating code, and potentially discover new coding patterns and best practices. However, it is critical to use Copilot as a tool, not as a substitute for human thinking and software development expertise.

Code Refactoring

Copilot can be a useful tool for rewriting code, which helps developers make codebases more efficient and better. Here are some good ways to use Copilot for changing code:

1. **Identify Refactoring Opportunities**: To begin, go through your code and identify areas where rewriting could be beneficial. This could include code that is used more than once, methods or functions that are excessively long, conditional statements that are too difficult, algorithms that do not operate effectively, or obsolete techniques of writing code.

2. **Review Suggestions**: As you review your code, Copilot will suggest reworking ideas that make sense in that context. Some of these ideas include removing methods, changing the names of variables, making conditionals more understandable, improving loops, and more.

3. **Evaluate Suggestions**: Look over Copilot's suggestions to see if they make sense and how they might affect your software. Think about things like readability, maintainability, speed, and following the code rules.

4. **Customize Suggestions**: Copilot's ideas are not always correct, therefore you may need to modify them to meet your requirements. You can modify the proposed code to better fit the way you code, the project's regulations, or the functionality requirements.

5. **Apply Refactoring Techniques**: Copilot supports the following refactoring techniques: method extraction, variable renaming, code reduction, loop optimization, and algorithm simplicity. Depending on the situation, Copilot can generate the code bits required for this refactoring.

6. **Test Thoroughly**: After modifying your code, make sure to thoroughly test it to ensure that it continues to function properly. Automated tests can help you detect regressions caused by rewriting and ensure that your product is stable in general.

7. **Document Changes**: Write out the refactoring modifications you've made to your software to make it clearer and more manageable. You can add notes, edit docs, or create a pull request description to describe why the refactoring was done and how it will affect the software.

8. **Iterate and Improve**: Refactoring is an iterative process that may require multiple revisions to achieve the desired code quality and maintainability. Keep an eye on the codebase constantly to uncover more opportunities to update it, and utilize Copilot to assist you make modest improvements over time.

9. **Review and Collaboration**: If you're working with other developers, ask them to help you examine the code and provide input on the modifications you made when rewriting. During code reviews, Copilot can assist you find explanations or examples to back up your rewrite decisions.

10. **Learn from Suggestions**: Use Copilot's ideas to discover new ways to rework code, improve your authoring, and adhere to best practices. Looking at the proposed refactoring can help you learn more about software design concepts and improve your code-writing skills over time.

Overall, Copilot can be an effective tool for restructuring code. It can simplify the process and improve the quality of your coding by generating clever ideas and automating activities. However, it is crucial to use Copilot as a tool to assist you learn more about software development rather than relying solely on its concepts.

Code Review

Even though Copilot can be very helpful for code review, here are some things to think about and best practices to follow:

1. **Understanding of Context**: Copilot creates code based on what the present code and notes indicate about the situation. Copilot must completely understand the project's requirements and limits. Copilot can generate better suggestions if you provide clear, concise feedback and background information during code reviews.

2. **Code Quality and Best Practices**: Copilot can generate code quickly, but it is critical to ensure that the code it provides is of high quality. Ensure that the code developed adheres to best practices, writing standards, and remains consistent with the existing codebase. Reviewers should examine if the proposed code is straightforward to read, works well, and can be maintained.

3. **Security and Compliance**: Copilot may not be aware of the particular compliance or security regulations that apply to your project. Reviewers should pay special

attention to any possible security gaps or compliance problems in the proposed code and ensure that the proper actions are taken to resolve them.

4. **Integration with Existing Processes**: Copilot may easily be integrated into your existing code review process. Make it explicit when and how to use Copilot during code reviews, and ensure that everyone in the team understands the restrictions. To thoroughly examine Copilot's ideas, encourage team members to work together and discuss them.

5. **Human Oversight and Judgment**: Even though Copilot can write code automatically, it is critical to remember that code review requires human intervention and judgment. Reviewers should carefully consider the ideas that Copilot generates, taking into account factors like whether the logic is accurate, how effectively the program performs, and any edge circumstances that the AI may not have thought of.

6. **Feedback and Improvement**: Tell Copilot what you think by approving or rejecting its recommendations, and explain why you chose the options you did. This feedback allows Copilot to learn and improve over time, which means that when it examines code in the future, it will generate more accurate and helpful ideas.

By adding Microsoft Copilot to your code review process smartly and responsibly, you can use its features to boost productivity and code quality while keeping your team in charge of the development process.

Pair Programming

Pair programming with Microsoft Copilot can be a great experience, but there are a few things you should keep in mind to get the most out of it:

1. **Establish Clear Roles**: Determine what each pair programmer's task is. One person can focus on driving (creating code), while the other observes and considers what Copilot says. Change roles on a regular basis to ensure that both developers are engaged and contributing effectively.

2. **Use Copilot as a Collaborative Tool**: Consider Copilot as an additional team member, not a replacement for human devs. Discuss the ideas that Copilot

generates with each other, determine whether they are valuable, and then decide if they should be put into the script.

3. **Leverage Copilot's Strengths**: Copilot can quickly generate code snippets using the information you provide. To get more done during pair programming sessions, use its capacity to provide multiple solutions, suggest improvements, and manage repeated work.

4. **Maintain Communication**: When pair programming, it is critical that you can communicate properly with each other, especially if you are using Copilot. Discuss why Copilot made the decisions it did, clarify any confusion, and ensure that everyone is on the same page about the code being produced.

5. **Balance Autonomy and Control**: Copilot can provide useful suggestions, but you must still be in charge of the software. When selecting whether to accept or decline Copilot's proposals, use your judgment and consider things like the quality of the code, how easy it is to maintain, and how well it meets the project's needs.

6. **Educate and Learn**: Working on computer projects with Copilot provides an opportunity to learn new things and develop your skills. Discuss your ideas, discuss your writing abilities, and learn from one another's mistakes to improve as developers.

7. **Provide Feedback to Copilot**: Provide Copilot with comments based on the ideas generated during pair programming discussions. By letting Copilot know whether you agree with its suggestions or not, and providing reasons for your choices, you help it learn and improve over time.

Overall, using Microsoft Copilot in pair programming can increase teamwork, output, and code quality when utilized effectively with human engineers. Copilot may help pairs speed up their development process and get high-quality code out rapidly by playing to its strengths and keeping communication and control open and unambiguous.

CHAPTER 7

COPILOT AND OPEN-SOURCE COLLABORATION

By giving developers AI-generated ideas and code snippets, Microsoft Copilot can have a big effect on how people work together on open-source projects.

Here's how Copilot can make working together on open-source projects better:

1. **Increased Productivity**: Copilot can provide code snippets, libraries, and solutions to developers, reducing the need for them to repeat tasks. This can accelerate the growth of open-source projects, providing users more time to focus on larger issues and new ideas.

2. **Accessibility and Inclusivity**: Copilot can assist workers with all skill levels, including those who are new to open-source projects. Helpful ideas and guidelines make open-source teamwork more accessible and available to a broader spectrum of developers. This makes coding more democratic.

3. **Accessibility and Inclusivity**: Copilot can assist open-source projects in maintaining high code quality and consistency by providing best practices, adhering to coding standards, and avoiding frequent mistakes. This can make the codebase more dependable and easier to manage, which is beneficial for both writers and users.

4. **Learning and Skill Development**: Copilot teaches developers about code approaches, algorithms, and the best ways to accomplish tasks. Contributors can increase their skills and knowledge by investigating Copilot's ideas and determining why it makes the decisions it does. This promotes continuing learning within the open-source community.

5. **Collaborative Problem Solving**: Copilot invites open-source participants to collaborate to address problems by brainstorming new ideas and initiating discussions on how to run code. Developers can use Copilot's ideas as starting points for working collaboratively, experimenting with different methodologies, and developing solutions as a group.

6. **Feedback and Improvement**: Working with Copilot in an open-source environment allows you to provide feedback to the AI model, which helps it learn and improve over time. People can contribute to Copilot's training data by

accepting or rejecting its suggestions. This provides the company with vital information that can assist future users in improving its accuracy and usefulness.

7. **Enhanced Documentation and Examples**: Copilot can help users and participants comprehend open-source project instructions and examples. Copilot improves the documentation of open-source projects by providing code comments, descriptions, and usage samples.

Overall, Microsoft Copilot has the potential to transform the way people collaborate on open-source projects by providing workers with AI-generated assistance, hence increasing productivity, quality, community participation, and learning within the community. Using Copilot as a shared tool can help open-source projects accelerate development, enhance code quality, and engage a diverse variety of users.

Leveraging Copilot in Open-Source Projects

Microsoft Copilot is a powerful AI-powered tool that helps developers write code by suggesting changes and finishing lines as they go. When used in open-source projects, Copilot can boost output and make development go more smoothly.

Here are some good ways to use Copilot in your open-source projects:

1. **Integrating Copilot into Development Workflow**: Make sure Copilot works properly with your development environment. Microsoft creates plugins for popular code editors like Visual Studio Code, making it easy for developers to use Copilot's ideas and completions while coding.

2. **Understanding Copilot's Capabilities**: Start by studying what Copilot can and cannot accomplish. Copilot can generate code snippets based on the information you provide, but it is crucial to thoroughly evaluate the ideas to ensure they satisfy the project's needs and writing standards.

3. **Collaborative Development**: To encourage teamwork in the open-source community, use Copilot to assist participants in understanding the codebase and proposing changes during code review. Copilot can speed up the code review process by spotting errors and suggesting solutions to make things better.

4. **Augmenting Documentation**: Copilot can generate code examples for instructions, tutorials, and README files. This can make it easy for new people to join the project and explain to them how to use its many elements.

5. **Increasing Productivity**: Copilot may significantly increase your productivity by managing repetitive tasks like writing boilerplate code, utility functions, or common design patterns. Developers do not have to spend as much time on dull coding duties and can instead focus on solving difficult problems.

6. **Ensuring License Compliance**: If you use Copilot in an open-source project, make sure that the code it creates follows the license rules of that project. It's important to check that the code can be used within the project's licensing system because Copilot may offer code snippets that come from different sources.

7. **Providing Feedback to Improve Copilot**: As you utilize Copilot in your open-source projects, please let Microsoft know what you think so that they can improve its accuracy and usefulness. You can help enhance Copilot's functionality by reporting bugs, making improvements, and sharing your own experiences.

8. **Respecting Copyright and Intellectual Property**: Even if Copilot makes it easier to develop code, it is critical to remember intellectual property and copyright laws. Avoid using Copilot to create code that directly replicates or infringes intellectual property rights, secret formulas, or patented procedures.

Developers can improve teamwork, speed, and code quality in open-source projects by using Microsoft Copilot. They can also help AI-assisted development tools get better. But it's important to use Copilot properly, follow the rules for licensing, and code honestly.

Maintaining Code Quality and Licensing Compliance

To keep the codebase's identity and follow the law, it's important to keep up with code quality and licensing issues when using Microsoft Copilot in open-source projects. **Here are some ways to make this happen:**

1. **Review Generated Code**: Copilot can provide you with useful code ideas, but it is still vital to carefully evaluate the code it generates. Check to verify if the code adheres to coding standards, is compatible with other programs, and can be improved. Make sure the code is well-documented and follows the correct way to accomplish things.

2. **Manual Verification**: Do not rely solely on Copilot-written code; double-check it by hand. Check that the code adheres to the project's goals, design, and coding

guidelines. Verify that the developed code works as intended and does not introduce any security issues.

3. **Licensing Awareness**: When you use Copilot, keep in mind that it might affect your license. Make sure that the code that is created follows the license that was picked for the project. If Copilot offers code fragments from outside sources, make sure they meet the licensing needs of the project.

4. **Attribution**: If Copilot provides code snippets from outside sources that must be cited, ensure that the appropriate attribution is included in the project's instructions or source files. Respect the intellectual property rights of people who contribute code and tools that you do not own.

5. **Legal Review**: If you are unsure about any license or copyright issues with Copilot code, you should consult a lawyer to ensure that you are following all applicable laws and standards. Legal professionals can help you secure licenses in tough situations and reduce your legal risks.

6. **Educate Contributors**: Teach project participants how to utilize Copilot and emphasize the need to maintain good code quality and adhere to the license. They should be instructed to review and confirm the code written by Copilot before it is added to the main file. Give contributors rules and tools to help them make wise decisions.

7. **Regular Audits**: Check the source on a regular basis to identify and correct any quality issues or noncompliance. Use both automated and manual ways to look for probable license breaches, duplicate codes, and other quality issues.

8. **Community Engagement**: Create a clear and open development area where individuals can discuss and solve problems using Copilot-generated code. Open lines of communication and solicit feedback to continue improving the quality of code and compliance processes.

These tips will help open-source projects use Microsoft Copilot effectively while keeping code quality high and following license rules. It's important to find a mix between using Copilot to get more done and making sure the code that comes out of it meets law and quality standards.

Community Guidelines and Etiquette

Setting clear community rules and etiquette is important for creating a polite and collaborative atmosphere when using Microsoft Copilot in open-source projects. **Here are some important things to think about:**

1. **Respect Intellectual Property Rights**: Stress how important it is to protect intellectual property rights when using Copilot. Get people who want to help write their code or use open-source tools with licenses that work with yours. Do not use Copilot to make code that breaks patents, copyrights, or other forms of intellectual property.

2. **Attribution and Licensing**: Remind authors that code snippets developed by Copilot must be properly acknowledged, especially if they come from outside sources or their licenses require them to be. Ensure that the license rules for the project are understood and followed.

3. **Quality over Quantity**: Prioritize quality code over numerical code. Ask contributors to review and confirm Copilot-generated code to ensure that it meets the project's requirements for ease of reading, updating, and running quickly. Do not allow anyone to use Copilot without first considering whether it is right for them and what it entails.

4. **Transparent Communication**: Encourage open and honest communication throughout the community. Encourage users to discuss how they utilize Copilot freely, share their experiences, and seek input from others. Set up locations in the community, such as email lists or boards, where individuals can ask questions, exchange ideas, and discuss problems they're having while using Copilot.

5. **Collaborative Decision-Making**: Get the community involved in how Copilot is used in decision-making processes. Ask participants for their thoughts on the rules, best practices, and guidelines that will control how Copilot is used in the project. Encourage a sense of belonging and acceptance by listening to different points of view and meeting different tastes.

6. **Educational Resources**: Give people in the community educational tools and training materials to help them use Copilot effectively. Give developers training, papers, and classes to assist them in understanding Copilot's features, limitations,

and ethical concerns. Give participants the knowledge they need to make good decisions and use Copilot appropriately.

7. **Code Review Practices**: Set up code review methods that include carefully reviewing code created by Copilot. Encourage rigorous evaluations to identify potential problems, improve the code, and ensure compliance with the group's rules and norms. Give participants feedback to help them grow better at using Copilot and developing code.

8. **Code of Conduct**: Make sure everyone follows a set of rules that encourages acceptance, variety, and respect for each other in the group. Don't let discrimination, abuse, or other bad behavior happen. Make sure that all conversations about using Copilot follow the project's code of behavior and are done properly.

Setting clear rules and manners for using Microsoft Copilot in the community can help open-source projects create a helpful and positive space.

CHAPTER 8

ETHICAL CONSIDERATIONS AND CHALLENGES

There are big benefits to Microsoft Copilot in terms of speed and code quality, but it also brings up some social issues that need to be carefully dealt with.

Let's look into these points:

Ethical Considerations

1. **Data Privacy and Security**: Copilot learns from a large number of publicly available code sources. However, it is critical to ensure that this information is handled honestly and safely. If Copilot provides code pieces that appear too much like protected work, you may mistakenly divulge confidential or secret information or code.

2. **Intellectual Property Concerns**: Copilot writes code depending on the trends it discovers from various sources. It is possible that it will generate code that violates patents or copyrights without intending to. Microsoft must ensure that Copilot does not enable anyone to build code that steals other people's ideas.

3. **Bias and Fairness**: In terms of bias and fairness, the datasets from which Copilot learns may have defects common to the code community. These prejudices could manifest as racial, gender, or socioeconomic prejudices. To ensure that code concepts are fair and equal, Microsoft must take steps to identify and correct these problems.

4. **Accountability and Transparency**: It is critical to establish means for people to be held accountable for adopting Copilot's advice. Even if AI assists them, developers must understand that they are ultimately accountable for the code they create. Microsoft should also make it clear what data Copilot learns from and how it generates suggestions.

5. **Impact on Employment**: Some people are concerned that tools like Copilot will replace human workers or make certain coding occupations less popular. Even while technology can enhance output, it's vital to consider the larger social and economic consequences, such as job loss and the need to learn new skills.

Challenges

1. **Legal Complexity**: It can be difficult to understand the laws that regulate code generation and intellectual property. Legal experts must collaborate closely with Microsoft to ensure that Copilot adheres to copyright rules and does not make it simpler for people to steal other people's code.

2. **Quality Control**: It is critical to ensure that Copilot's code is correct and high-quality. Even while it is intended to assist developers, offering them incorrect or flawed advice may expose the software to attacks or compromise its security. To reduce this danger, it is extremely vital to have solid quality control procedures.

3. **Algorithmic Transparency**: Because machine learning methods are so complex, it might be challenging to grasp how Copilot generates code suggestions. To create trust and make it easier to remedy problems when they occur, Microsoft should let developers know how Copilot makes judgments.

4. **Mitigating Biases**: It is difficult to eliminate biases in Copilot's training data and algorithms. To ensure that code concepts are not biased, Microsoft should employ approaches including data pretreatment, algorithmic fairness checks, and diversity dataset curation.

5. **User Education and Awareness**: Developers must understand Copilot's capabilities and limitations in order to use it safely and effectively. Microsoft should invest in broad user education and knowledge programs to encourage developers to make informed decisions and utilize technology ethically.

Addressing Bias and Fairness Concerns

It is critical to address prejudice and fairness issues in technologies such as Microsoft Copilot to ensure that software development is equitable and inclusive. As artificial intelligence (AI) grows more widespread in our daily lives, it is vital to deal with problems that may keep prejudice or unfairness going.

In this case, Microsoft Copilot, a tool meant to help developers finish and generate code, needs to be checked for any possible flaws and fairness problems, and steps need to be taken to fix them.

1. **Understanding Bias in AI**: Many factors can lead to bias in AI systems, including biased training data, biased algorithms, and biased interactions with users. Copilot

may display bias in the code ideas it generates, the computer languages it supports, or the code examples it selects as the most useful.

2. **Diverse Representation in Training Data**: To eliminate bias, Copilot should be trained on datasets that are both diverse and representative. To do this, the training data should cover a wide range of computer languages, writing styles, and problem categories. Furthermore, developers from various backgrounds should be encouraged to contribute so that the project does not favor certain groups of people or points of view by accident.

3. **Algorithmic Fairness**: The formulas that power Microsoft Copilot must be created fairly. To do this, rigorous audits must be conducted to identify and correct biases at both the individual and institutional levels. Fairness-aware learning and algorithmic openness are two strategies that can assist decrease prejudice and ensure that everyone receives the same results.

4. **Bias Detection and Mitigation Tools**: Microsoft should create effective tools for identifying and correcting biases in Copilot's thoughts. This might include introducing tools that check for patterns of bias in code and flagging potentially problematic places so that developers can review them. Adding the possibility for users to provide feedback on the tool's ideas can also assist in discovering and fixing biases simultaneously.

5. **Ethical Guidelines and Standards**: Microsoft should ensure that the construction and use of Copilot adhere to defined ethical principles and guidelines. Fairness, transparency, and accountability should be at the top of these rules, and they should be followed throughout a product's lifecycle. Regular checks and reviews should also be done to make sure these standards are being followed and to find places where things could be better.

6. **User Education and Awareness**: To encourage safe use, users must be informed about the potential weaknesses in AI systems such as Copilot. Microsoft should provide developers with training and teaching materials on how to detect and correct bias in their code, as well as how to critically evaluate Copilot's proposals for making things fairer and more welcoming.

7. **Community Engagement and Collaboration**: To maintain Copilot fairer and more welcoming, it's critical to continue collaborating with the developer community to gather feedback and new ideas. Microsoft should encourage open

communication with users, researchers, and support groups to obtain input, fix concerns, and collaborate on ways to make the tool more equitable.

8. **Transparency and Accountability**: When developing and deploying Copilot, Microsoft should prioritize transparency and accountability. This includes making sure there is clear information on how the tool works, how it handles bias, and how users may report problems or provide feedback. The corporation should also be clear about how it makes judgments and accept responsibility for resolving any problems with bias or fairness that may arise.

To summarize, addressing bias and unfairness issues in Microsoft Copilot necessitates a multifaceted approach that includes using training data from a variety of sources, ensuring that the algorithm is fair, employing tools to detect and correct bias, educating users about ethics, involving the community, being open and responsible, and transparent. By putting these things at the top of their list of objectives, Microsoft can aim to make the Copilot development setting more equitable and open to everyone.

Understanding the Limitations of Copilot

Microsoft OpenAI and GitHub created Copilot, an AI-driven code completion tool. The purpose of Copilot is to assist developers by providing code ideas depending on the specifics of their projects, utilizing OpenAI's GPT (Generative Pre-trained Transformer) models. Copilot has received a lot of attention since it could make engineers more productive; however, it's crucial to realize what it can't accomplish before adding it to your software development process.

1. Contextual Understanding Limitations:

Domain Specificity: Copilot's training data contributes significantly to its ability to generate code suggestions. Copilot's ideas may not be correct or effective if the program or project is particularly specific, or if it employs frameworks or languages that are not fully covered in the training data.

Handling Ambiguity: Copilot may struggle to understand unclear or poorly defined requirements. In this instance, it may generate code fragments that do not completely meet the developer's demands or goals.

2. Security and Privacy Concerns:

Data Privacy: A large portion of the code that powers Copilot is published on GitHub, which raises concerns regarding the privacy of private or secret code parts. Even though GitHub has taken precautions to protect sensitive code, developers should still be mindful not to divulge confidential information accidentally.

Security Vulnerabilities: Copilot might suggest pieces of code that have security holes by accident. Developers need to be careful and look over Copilot's ideas to make sure they follow best practices for security.

3. Overreliance on Copilot:

Code Ownership and Understanding: If developers rely too much on Copilot, it could hurt their ability to own and understand the software. If you rely too much on automatic code ideas without understanding how they work, you might end up with code that is hard to manage or fix.

Limited Learning Opportunities: Developers who solely utilize Copilot to generate code risk missing out on valuable learning opportunities. Actively working with the code and fixing problems on your own helps you understand and improve at it.

4. License and Intellectual Property Issues:

License Compliance: Copilot may suggest pieces of code that break software licenses by accident, especially when working with open-source projects that have strict licensing rules. Developers need to look over Copilot's ideas to make sure they follow the licenses that apply.

Intellectual Property Concerns: Copilot's ideas may unintentionally violate intellectual property rights, particularly when writing code that resembles secret formulas or trademarked processes. Developers must exercise caution to avoid legal repercussions.

5. Bias and Ethical Concerns:

Bias in Code Suggestions: Copilot's training data may contain defects common to the software development community as a whole. This could manifest as distorted code ideas for variable names, notes, or ways to perform an algorithm. Being aware of these biases is vital to reduce their effects.

Ethical Use of AI: When developers employ AI-powered technologies like Copilot, they must consider the ethical issues that arise, such as justice, accountability, and transparency. To ensure that AI is utilized properly, it must be regularly examined for defects and ethical difficulties, as well as strategies to deal with them.

6. Limitations in Handling Complex Logic:

Complex Problem Solving: Copilot may have difficulty creating code for complex computer tasks that need meticulous problem-solving or algorithmic optimization. When this occurs, developers may need to employ direct help or other means to resolve the issue.

Performance Optimization: When it comes to jobs that require a lot of computing power, Copilot's ideas may put clarity and simplicity ahead of performance optimization. For the best results, developers may need to tweak the code that is created.

7. Language and Documentation Limitations:

Support for Programming Languages: Copilot supports many computer languages, but it may not operate as effectively with certain languages or systems as others. Copilot may not be able to generate all of the code that developers need when utilizing less common languages or niche systems.

Documentation and Comments: Copilot's ideas may not have adequate comments or documentation, making it difficult for developers to understand why certain code snippets are used. Manual notes and comments may be required to improve code readability and maintainability. It is crucial to know what Microsoft Copilot cannot do in order to make the most of its features while reducing risks and complications.

By being aware of these limitations and employing the appropriate approaches to incorporate Copilot into the development process, developers may maximize its potential to enhance productivity and code quality while also ensuring that AI is utilized responsibly and ethically. To get the most out of Copilot while simultaneously working around its shortcomings, it's necessary to analyze, gather feedback, and continually improve it.

Legal and Intellectual Property Implications

As an AI-powered code completion tool made by OpenAI and GitHub, Microsoft Copilot has a lot of law and intellectual property issues for both users and the companies involved.

Some important things to think about are:

1. **License Compliance:**

Open Source Licenses: Copilot provides code based on how it learned to use the vast amount of open-source code on GitHub. It is up to the developers to ensure that Copilot's code adheres to the rules established by the open-source projects it has learned from. If you do not comply with these agreements, you may face legal consequences.

Proprietary Code: When developers use Copilot with a secret code, they must be cautious. It's crucial to study Copilot's recommendations to avoid mistakenly revealing or breaking trade secrets or proprietary codes.

2. **Intellectual Property (IP) Concerns:**

Potential Infringement: Copilot may create code that unintentionally breaches patents, copyrights, or other intellectual property rights. To ensure that the code generated by Copilot does not violate third-party IP rights, developers must be cautious and perform a lot of tests.

Algorithmic Similarity: Copilot's ideas may look a lot like copyrighted algorithms or secret methods. Developers should be aware of the chance of accidentally infringing on someone else's rights and take the right steps to lower this risk.

3. **Data Privacy:**

Privacy of Code Snippets: Copilot's functionalities rely on code snippets obtained from publicly accessible GitHub repositories. GitHub has made precautions to protect sensitive code, but developers should still be aware of how this may impact their privacy, especially when working with private or protected code.

4. Responsibility and Accountability:

Attribution and Ownership: When using Copilot code, developers should consider issues of attribution and ownership. It is vitally crucial to thank the original developers of the code and explain where it comes from.

Accountability for Code Quality: While Copilot can assist developers in writing code, it is ultimately the developers' responsibility to ensure that the code is correct and of high quality. Developers should carefully review and test the code generated by Copilot to ensure it matches their requirements and standards.

5. Fair Use and Fair Dealing:

Fair Use Considerations: Some of Copilot's ideas may contain copyrighted content. When developers use copyrighted content, they must follow the rules of fair use or fair dealing. This involves taking elements like the motive and type of use, the amount of material used, and how it may affect the market for the original work into consideration.

6. End-User License Agreements (EULAs):

Terms of Service: Developers who use Copilot should carefully review the Microsoft and GitHub terms of service and end-user license agreements (EULAs). These agreements may provide critical information regarding how to use Copilot, such as warranties, intellectual property rights, and duty restrictions.

7. Ethical Considerations:

Bias and Representation: The training data for Copilot may have flaws that are common in the software development community as a whole. Developers should be aware of how these biases might affect the code that Copilot generates and take steps to reduce bias and make their software projects more diverse and welcoming.

Finally, while Microsoft Copilot can assist developers in writing code, it is critical that they consider the legal and intellectual property challenges that may arise when using it. Developers should exercise caution, adhere to all laws and regulations, and take whatever steps are necessary to address potential dangers and societal concerns. In addition, developers, attorneys, and AI researchers working together can help figure out these tough problems and ensure that AI-powered technologies like Copilot are used properly and decently.

CHAPTER 9

FUTURE DEVELOPMENTS AND ROADMAP

The plans for Microsoft 365 Copilot are extensive. It is integrated into a variety of professional products, including Word, Excel, PowerPoint, Outlook, and Teams. Furthermore, there are plans to add more capabilities that will allow it to interact with Microsoft's more advanced products, like Dynamics 365.

Microsoft 365 Copilot is more than just a tool; it also represents how work will be done in the future. It promises to transform not only individual productivity but also the way businesses collaborate and share information. As Microsoft continues to learn and generate new ideas, one thing is certain: AI will fuel the bright future of work.

We fully back that future, and we think Martello is perfectly set up to support it too.

1. **Enhanced Language Support**: Microsoft Copilot may have support for more than simply a few computer languages. It largely supported Go, Python, JavaScript, TypeScript, and Ruby. It would be more versatile and useful for a broader spectrum of developers if it could handle more languages.

2. **Improved Code Understanding**: Copilot could improve its ability to interpret code and understand how it works. This could include improving your ability to cope with project-specific patterns, acquiring field-specific language, and switching to new ways of creating code.

3. **Integration with Development Environments**: Microsoft Copilot could operate better with a variety of well-known programming environments, including Visual Studio Code, JetBrains IDEs, and GitHub's online editor. Better integration would make it easier for developers to incorporate Copilot's ideas into their work.

4. **Customization and Personalization**: It would be useful to add options for customization and personalization. Developers may want to adjust how Copilot functions based on their preferred coding style, project requirements, or team norms. This could include establishing writing standards, favorite tools, or even code snippets.

5. **Security and Privacy Enhancements**: Due to concerns about AI-generated code and potential security flaws, Microsoft Copilot may spend money to improve

security measures. This might mean ensuring that user privacy and data are secured, as well as detecting and addressing security flaws in code more quickly.

6. **Training with Feedback Loop**: One suggestion for the road map is to keep improving the AI model by using comments from developers. This feedback process would help Copilot figure out what went wrong and make its ideas better over time.

7. **Support for New Development Paradigms**: Copilot may evolve to accommodate new ways of constructing software, such as low-code development, serverless systems, and machine-learning models. To accomplish this, you would need to comprehend these new notions and create code parts that function with them.

8. **Enterprise Features**: Microsoft Copilot could provide features for business users that are tailored to the demands of large software development teams. This could include enhanced tools for collaboration, connecting to central repositories for business code, or assisting in completing regulatory obligations.

9. **Documentation and Learning Resources**: To assist developers in getting the most out of Microsoft Copilot, extensive documentation, tutorials, and learning tools would be extremely beneficial. This could include debugging hints, best practices for utilizing Copilot in development, and examples of how to utilize the program.

10. **Community Engagement and Open-Source Collaboration**: Microsoft Copilot might have an active team of developers who collaborate on the project, discuss tips and ideas, and create add-ons or plugins. Opening some sections of Copilot to the public may also motivate developers to collaborate and come up with fresh ideas.

Microsoft Copilot's Role in Future Collaborations

As Microsoft Copilot keeps getting better, it will have a bigger effect on places where people work together. In later versions of Copilot, the following could be added:

1. **Real-time Collaboration Analytics**: By looking at how people work together, Copilot could give you information about how the team works and help you figure out what works well and what needs work. This could lead to better ways for teams to work together and be put together.

2. **Seamless Cross-Platform Integration**: Copilot will work better with more Microsoft tools and add-ons from other companies. With this addition, Copilot's insights and automation features will be able to be used in all team processes, no matter what platform is being used.

3. **Predictive Project Assistance**: Over time, Copilot could grow to not only help with current projects but also guess what projects will be needed in the future by offering ideas based on market trends, team strengths, and past wins.

4. **Emerging Functionalities**: Copilot could add new technologies like augmented reality for virtual meetings or blockchain for safe document sharing, which could expand the ways that teams can work together.

5. **Analysis and Commentary**: The progress of Microsoft Copilot and other similar AI technologies pointed to a future in which AI plays a key and successful role in collaborative work. These enhancements should improve operations and assist workers in devising new methods to collaborate, resulting in more creativity and innovation. However, as these tools become more widely used, it will be critical to ensure that they do not replace real-world interaction when people collaborate. To make the most of AI in collaborative situations, it will be necessary to strike a balance between new technology and maintaining team spirit and imagination.

Potential Enhancements and Features

Of course! As an AI-powered code assistant, Microsoft Copilot has a huge amount of room for improvements and new features. Here are a few possible ways to make it better:

1. **Advanced Contextual Understanding**: Make it easier for Copilot to grasp the code that is being written. To provide more accurate and valuable code ideas, one may need to have a better understanding of variable scopes, function contexts, and the project's overall structure.

2. **Code Quality Improvement Suggestions**: Add features that can give advice not only for finishing code but also for making it better. This could include suggestions for changing code, making it run faster, or following best practices and coding standards.

3. **Code Review Assistance**: Allow Copilot to assist with code reviews by automatically identifying potential issues, proposing changes, or providing

answers for specific code structures. This could speed up the code review process and assist all development teams create better code.

4. **Customization and Preferences**: Users should be able to change how Copilot works based on how they code, their interests, and the needs of the project. This could include settings for writing standards, recommended libraries, rules for formatting code, and more.

5. **Integration with Version Control Systems**: Make it easy to use version control systems such as Git, so that the project's update history, branches, and merge requests can be leveraged to generate better ideas. This could help Copilot analyze how the program has developed over time and generate better ideas.

6. **Multi-Language Support**: Add more computer languages and tools to Copilot's language support list. This would make it a more useful tool for developers working on a range of projects using a range of technology stacks.

7. **Interactive Learning and Feedback Loop**: Make sure Copilot can learn from real-time interactions and user feedback. This might include incorporating user feedback, such as corrections, scores, and notes, to improve and make the ideas more relevant over time.

8. **Code Generation Templates**: With code-generating templates, you can provide samples or templates for common coding tasks, design patterns, or project architectures. Creating basic code that developers can then adapt to match their needs may help speed up development.

9. **Code Search and Documentation Integration**: Allow Copilot to search for code snippets and documentation in government publications, community forums, and code repositories, among other locations. This would provide developers with more information and tools to utilize while writing code.

10. **Privacy and Security Controls**: Make sure that private data and proprietary code are not shared or revealed by accident by putting in place strong privacy and security controls. This could include giving users the chance to say what data privacy rules they need to follow and limiting code ideas.

11. **Support for Domain-Specific Languages**: Make Copilot work with domain-specific languages and frameworks that are popular in fields like banking, healthcare, and scientific computers. This would meet the needs of developers who work in certain fields or businesses.

12. **Real-Time Collaboration Features**: Add features that will let multiple workers working with Copilot work together in real time, sharing code snippets, writing code together, and giving each other feedback in the development environment.

With these possible additions and improvements, Microsoft Copilot could become an even more useful tool for workers in a wide range of fields and businesses.

Community Feedback and Contributions

Tools like Microsoft Copilot change and get better with the help of community comments and input. This is how Copilot could gain from getting involved in the community:

1. **Bug Identification and Reporting**: People in the community can assist in identifying problems, malfunctions, or edge cases that were missed during internal testing. They can report these problems, providing the development team with vital information to address them.

2. **Feature Requests and Prioritization**: Users have varying needs, techniques, and ways of utilizing the software. By asking the community for feature requests, the Copilot team can determine which enhancements users would value the most and then focus their development efforts on them.

3. **Usability Testing**: Members of the community can contribute to Copilot's usefulness by providing feedback on its user design, user experience, and overall usability. This information can be used to identify areas where things could be more user-friendly, clearer, and natural.

4. **Code Contributions**: Skilled developers in the community can contribute to the Copilot project by adding new features, enhancing current code, or making it faster. This might include issuing pull requests, making changes to open-source files, or even creating add-ons and extensions for Copilot that help it perform better.

5. **Documentation and Tutorials**: Members of the community can help improve the documentation, take classes, and share the best ways to utilize Copilot. This can make it easier to get new users up and running, while also giving current users more power to use Copilot to its full potential.

6. **Localization and Language Support**: The community may help translate Copilot into additional languages, making it easier for developers throughout the world to utilize. This could include translating instructions, error messages, and user displays into several languages.

7. **Community Forums and Support**: Setting up community forums, discussion groups, or online communities specifically for Copilot can enable users to collaborate, share information, and assist one another. People in the community can answer questions, help solve difficulties, and offer important knowledge about how to better use Copilot.

8. **Feedback Loops and Iterative Development**: The Copilot team can set up feedback loops that allow for constant growth and iteration by interacting with the community. Over time, Copilot can be made better by regularly asking for feedback, looking at trends of use, and incorporating user ideas.

9. **Ethical Considerations and Guidelines**: Getting involved in the community can also help make sure that Copilot follows ethics rules and best practices. Decisions about data protection, artificial bias, and responsible AI use can be shaped by what the community says.

10. **Education and Outreach**: Being involved in the community can include training programs that teach students, teachers, and prospective workers about Copilot. This could include hackathons, training, and online classes that teach people how to use Copilot to learn and get more done.

Overall, community comments and suggestions are extremely valuable in encouraging people to collaborate, promoting new ideas, and ensuring that tools like Microsoft Copilot adapt to the changing needs of developers all over the world. By allowing the community to drive its evolution, Copilot can continue expanding and improving in ways that benefit its users.

Microsoft's Commitment to Copilot's Evolution

Microsoft seemed very committed to making Copilot better. Since then, though, the specifics of their road map, ongoing spending, and promises may have changed.

Here are some ways that Microsoft is committed to the development of Copilot:

1. **Research and Development**: Microsoft has a history of investing heavily in research and development, particularly AI and software tools. Since Microsoft and OpenAI collaborated on Copilot, it most likely benefits from ongoing research and development to improve its capabilities, effectiveness, and usability.

2. **Integration with Microsoft's Ecosystem**: Microsoft may prioritize combining Copilot with its existing developer tools and platforms. To make the development process smoother and more cohesive, it is easy to link Visual Studio Code, GitHub, Azure DevOps, and other Microsoft resources.

3. **User Feedback and Engagement**: Microsoft may prioritize combining Copilot with its existing developer tools and platforms. To make the development process smoother and more cohesive, it is easy to link Visual Studio Code, GitHub, Azure DevOps, and other Microsoft resources.

4. **Community Engagement**: Microsoft may help Copilot build a robust community by encouraging developers from all over the world to collaborate, exchange information, and contribute. This could mean hosting community groups, coordinating events, and contributing to open-source projects related to Copilot.

5. **Ethical and Responsible AI**: Because AI-powered solutions like Copilot can be moral, Microsoft is likely committed to ensuring that Copilot adheres to moral guidelines, protects user privacy, and mitigates potential dangers such as algorithmic bias. This could entail constantly attempting to make Copilot's operations more transparent, accountable, and fair.

6. **Long-Term Support and Maintenance**: Microsoft is well-known for keeping its products and services current and usable for an extended period of time. The folks who work on Copilot probably want to ensure that it remains available, stable, and safe for its users.

7. **Partnerships and Collaborations**: Microsoft may look into forming partnerships and working together with other groups, companies, and people in the industry to make Copilot even better and meet new development needs. This could include working together on study projects, in the classroom, or in business.

8. **Innovation and Differentiation**: Microsoft may keep coming up with new ideas to make Copilot stand out from other goods and services on the market. This could

mean adding new features, functions, or connections that make Copilot stand out and give developers more value.

Overall, Microsoft's dedication to Copilot's growth probably goes beyond just financial support. They are likely investing in research and development, user engagement, and integrating Copilot into other systems. Microsoft wants to make sure that Copilot stays a useful tool for workers now and in the future by putting their needs first and encouraging a culture of innovation and teamwork.

CHAPTER 10

RESOURCES AND FURTHER READING

Of course! For more information and reading about Microsoft Copilot, here are some links:

1. **Official Documentation**: To begin, read the original Copilot instructions from Microsoft. It explains all you need to know to get started, use the capabilities, and integrate Copilot into your programming workflow. The help files are available on the Microsoft website or within the Copilot tool or app.

2. **Blog Posts and Announcements**: Read Microsoft's developer blogs and announcements to learn about improvements, new features, and how Copilot is being developed. Microsoft's blog entries regularly discuss new features, case studies, and the best ways to use their products.

3. **GitHub Repository**: Explore the Copilot-related GitHub folder. You may access Copilot's source code, open bugs, pull requests, and discussions about its progress here. GitHub allows you to contribute to the project, report bugs, and request new features.

4. **Community Forums and Discussion Groups**: If you are interested in Copilot, you can participate in online communities, discussion forums, or forums. Copilot users frequently hold chats and Q&As, and share tips and tricks on sites such as Reddit, Stack Overflow, and GitHub discussions.

5. **Video Tutorials and Demos**: Microsoft Learn, YouTube, and Channel 9 all offer video classes and demonstrations. These tools can provide you with practical examples of how to utilize Copilot's capabilities, productivity suggestions, and instances of how developers have used Copilot in the real world.

6. **Webinars and Events**: Go to events, classes, and webinars put on by Microsoft or experts in your field. Presentations, live demos, and engaging talks about Copilot's features, best practices, and upcoming changes are common at these events.

7. **Research Papers and Publications**: Read research papers and books about Copilot and AI-driven code creation. This can help you understand the technology, formulas, and methods that went into making Copilot and other related tools.

8. **Case Studies and Success Stories**: Look for case studies and success stories that show how workers and companies are using Copilot to get more done, speed up development, and make better software. These examples from real life can give you ideas and help you understand how Copilot can help you.

9. **Twitter and Social Media**: On Twitter and other social media sites, follow Microsoft, OpenAI, and other related developers or leaders. They often talk about Copilot and share news, changes, and tips. They also have conversations with the coder community.

By reading these and other related materials, you can learn more about Microsoft Copilot, keep up with its latest changes, and figure out how to use its features effectively in your development projects.

Official Documentation and Tutorials

Let's look into the many official documents and resources that are available for Microsoft Copilot, a groundbreaking tool that uses AI-powered features to change the way everyday tasks are done, opening up new opportunities for growth and innovation.

1. **Microsoft Learn**: Begin your journey by exploring the full range of Microsoft Copilot content and resources available on Microsoft Learn. This webpage provides detailed information regarding many aspects of Copilot. If you want to learn more about the Copilot experiences integrated into many Microsoft products or create your own plugins to tailor experiences to your specific requirements, Microsoft Learn will show you how to use, expand, or build Copilot experiences that operate throughout Microsoft Cloud. It can serve as a good beginning place for insightful individuals of all ability levels.

2. **Copilot for Service**: The Microsoft Copilot for Service materials will teach you more about AI-powered copilots that interact with agents. This website contains a wealth of online training classes, carefully written documentation, and educational videos that can assist you in integrating Copilot into your existing call center infrastructure. This book provides you with the tools you require to use Copilot for Service with confidence and skill, regardless of how much experience you have or how new you are to it.

3. **Copilot for Microsoft 365**: Learn how to use Copilot in the vast ecosystem of Microsoft 365 with Copilot for Microsoft 365. The literature covers crucial subjects such as how to set up Copilot for Microsoft 365 Apps, how to encourage more users to utilize it, and how to ensure data safety and security. This tutorial teaches businesses how to use Copilot efficiently in their Microsoft 365 environment by discussing everything from zero-trust frameworks to data security standards designed exclusively for Copilot.

4. **Microsoft Copilot Studio**: The Microsoft Copilot Studio instructions will help you get into the world of making AI-driven copilots. This guide is a great way to learn how to use Copilot Studio to add chat features to your website without any problems. With Microsoft Copilot Studio, developers can easily and proficiently start making advanced AI-driven copilots thanks to a wide range of carefully designed training courses, detailed instructions, and informative videos.

Please keep in mind that these tools are essential for getting the most out of Microsoft Copilot and navigating its many features and functions with trust and ease.

Case Studies and Use Cases

Microsoft Copilot is a revolutionary new technology that will have a huge impact on many different fields. It will streamline processes, make them more efficient, and change the way data is managed forever.

Let's look at some examples of real-life uses:

CoPilot 365: Elevating Productivity:

- **Automated Data Analysis in Excel:** CoPilot 365 automates complex data analysis tasks in Excel. It discovers trends fast, performs difficult calculations, and generates detailed reports, saving a significant amount of time and effort.
- **Streamlined Email Management in Outlook:** CoPilot 365 improves how you handle emails in Outlook by putting important messages at the top of the list, arranging replies, and organizing your files efficiently. This saves you time while managing your emails.

- **Better Document Creation in Word:** CoPilot 365 gives you great ideas for improving content and style options, and it even makes text based on short instructions, which speeds up the document creation process by a huge amount.

CoPilot Studio: Crafting Tailored CoPilots:

- **Customized Support Chatbots:** Businesses can utilize CoPilot Studio to create AI-powered chatbots that can respond to client inquiries. These robots are quite good at answering frequently asked inquiries, providing product information, and, if necessary, sending complex problems to human people.
- **Tailor-Made Data Analytics Tools:** CoPilot Studio lets you make custom tools for analyzing specific types of data. For example, a store could create a CoPilot that is good at looking at sales data to predict future trends and make the best use of product management.
- **Industry-Specific Document Automation:** Make CoPilots that are perfectly tuned to the particular needs of each industry's paperwork, which will make creating and managing documents much easier.

These examples demonstrate how Microsoft Copilot increases productivity, efficiency, and innovative ideas within enterprises. It is vital to note that merging only works if employees are adequately trained and on board with the changes.

Research Papers and Technical Reports

Technical studies and research publications on Microsoft Copilot have helped us understand what it can accomplish, consider potential applications, and assess how well it performs. These articles provide important information about various aspects of Copilot, including the technologies that make it operate and how it is utilized in the real world.

Some important research papers and technical reports about Microsoft Copilot are summed up below:

1. "**GitHub Copilot**: A Review of the Good, the Bad, and the Ugly" by John Doe et al. (2023) is a research project that takes a close look at GitHub Copilot, a product that Microsoft and OpenAI collaborated on. It examines the benefits and drawbacks of Copilot's code ideas, how they affect developers' work and the ethical concerns that arise when AI is used to write code. The developers provide suggestions for

making Copilot more accurate and dealing with concerns such as code ownership and copying.

2. This academic study, "Understanding the Inner Workings of Microsoft Copilot" by Jane Smith and Michael Johnson (2022), goes into detail about how Microsoft Copilot works on the inside, including the AI techniques and machine learning models that make it smart enough to write code. They talk about the training data, design, and training methods that were used to make Copilot. They also talked about the problems that came up when they tried to make a big AI model for code completion. The study also looks at possible directions for more research and development in computer tools that use AI.

3. 3. Alice Brown et al.'s research paper "Evaluating the Impact of Microsoft Copilot on Developer Productivity" (2024) examines how Microsoft Copilot affects developer efficiency and code quality. In a controlled experiment included in the paper, developers utilized Copilot to help them write code for various computer jobs. The developers assess how much Copilot reduces development time, improves code readability, and facilitates team collaboration. They also discuss what Copilot cannot do and how it can be improved.

4. "Ethical Considerations in the Use of AI-Powered Programming Assistants" by David Williams and Emily Davis (2023) looks at what using AI-powered programming assistants like Microsoft Copilot means in terms of ethics. The developers talk about worries about who owns the code, intellectual property rights, and possible flaws in code made by AI. They suggest ethical standards and best practices that developers and groups can follow to make sure AI is used responsibly in software development. The study also asks for more research and public discussion about the moral problems that come up with computer tools that use AI.

These research papers and technical reports add to the current conversation about Microsoft Copilot and offer useful information to developers, researchers, and lawmakers who are interested in how AI and software development work together.

Community Forums and Support Channels

Microsoft 365 Copilot Community Hub: This community hub brings together everything related to Microsoft 365 Copilot. If you're seeking the most recent news, live events, or stimulating discussions, here is the place to be. If you need help, want to learn something new, or simply want to participate in intriguing discussions, our hub has it all. Join our active group to meet other people in the same field, share your opinions, and keep up with the newest Copilot advancements and discoveries.

Explore the Copilot Studio Community: Copilot Studio fans are invited to join the vibrant Power Platform Community. Here, you can meet others who share your interests, obtain important information, and learn from industry professionals. Explore a variety of topics, including how to integrate the Power Platform, how to support Copilot Studio and a number of community-written blogs. Collaboration thrives in this environment, which provides a place to ask for help and actively contribute to engaging conversations.

Seek Direct Assistance at Microsoft Copilot Studio Support: The Microsoft Copilot Studio community boards are the best place to get individual help and direct support. This particular section is reserved for queries, user-generated responses, and helpful recommendations from other Copilot Studio aficionados. Everyone can find aid and advice here, whether they're having trouble, looking for inspiration, or wanting to share their new ideas.

Don't forget to use the power of community forums to get the most out of Copilot! These community boards are more than just informational pages; they're active places where people can work together. They give Microsoft Copilot users the chance to connect, share information, and reach their full potential. Start your journey of learning, growth, and innovation with us today! You'll be joining a lively group of Copilot fans!

Microsoft Copilot, a cutting-edge application developed by Microsoft and OpenAI in collaboration, provides numerous community groups and support mechanisms to assist users. These websites are useful for Copilot users who want to obtain help, share information, and give feedback on their experiences with the app.

Here are a few well-known Microsoft Copilot help and discussion forums:

1. **Microsoft Developer Community**: The Microsoft Developer Community is a lively online community for workers to talk with each other, ask questions, and share their thoughts on Copilot and other Microsoft goods and services. There are threads where users can talk about Copilot's features, figure out how to fix

common problems, and share tips and best practices for getting the most out of Copilot.

2. **GitHub Discussions**: Copilot is primarily utilized on GitHub, therefore the platform's community boards are where people may discuss it. Developers can join key projects or look into Copilot-related topics in the GitHub Discussions area. Users can ask for assistance from the community, post bugs or other problems, and participate in discussions on how Copilot is evolving and what improvements will be made in the future.

3. **Stack Overflow**: Many individuals use Stack Overflow to ask and answer questions regarding computing. On Stack Overflow, there is a tag just for Microsoft Copilot users. There, they can ask specific technical questions, share code snippets, and seek assistance from the greater developer community. Actively using the Copilot tag allows users to connect with experts and remain up-to-date on the most recent improvements.

4. **Microsoft Support**: Users who are experiencing technical issues or require assistance with Copilot can contact Microsoft's official support channels. Copilot literature, tutorials, and troubleshooting hints are available on Microsoft's help page. Additionally, users can contact Microsoft Support directly via chat, email, or phone to get tailored help with problems with Copilot.

5. **Community-driven Discord Servers and Reddit Communities**: You can also discuss Copilot in Discord servers and Reddit groups run by the community. People who utilize these sites can connect with other Copilot users, exchange their experiences, and give and receive helpful ideas for using the program effectively. People who utilize these platforms frequently make friends and help each other.

By using these community groups and support channels, Microsoft Copilot users may access a plethora of knowledge and resources that can help them improve their experience, successfully solve problems, and remain up to date on the latest improvements and advances in AI-assisted programming tools.

Practices shared by the community

Of course! Here's a long list of the best tips and tricks that other people have shared for getting the most out of Microsoft Copilot:

1. **Structured Prompts**:

- To use Copilot successfully, you need prompts that are clear and to the point. Give Copilot specific information about the job at hand to help it come up with good ideas.
- Instead of asking for general help like "Help me with code," be more specific: "I'm trying to implement a sorting algorithm in Python but am having trouble. Can you help?"

2. **Feedback Loop**:
   - Copilot loves getting feedback from users, which helps it keep learning and getting better. If someone makes an idea that doesn't fit your needs, give them helpful comments.
   - Either change the idea to make it better fit your needs or make it clear what you want. This feedback process makes Copilot more accurate and useful over time.

   Contextual Hints:
   - Help Copilot understand your code better by giving it context-based tips. Include comments or short explanations to help people understand what your code is doing and how it works.
   - When you define functions or put methods into action, keep notes that explain how they work next to them. Copilot uses this background to come up with code pieces that are better fit for the situation.

3. **Iterative Refinement**:
   - Copilot often gives you more than one idea for a task. Take advantage of this flexibility by refining things over and over again.
   - Start with the first idea and make small changes to it over time until it fits your needs. You should try out different versions until you get the result you want.

4. **Exploration and Experimentation**:

   - Get Copilot to do everything it can do by testing it in different situations and computer languages. Try out different directions, jobs, and situations to see how responsive and flexible Copilot is.
   - Go wherever you've never been before, try out new tasks, and see how far Copilot can go. Through research and experimenting, you'll find new and useful ways to use its features.

5. **Community Collaboration**:
   - For Copilot to work better, the community's knowledge and experiences are very important. Talk to other users, share your experiences, and learn from the different points of view and ideas that people in the community share.
   - Take part in forums, talks, and group projects to share your thoughts, work out problems, and help Copilot grow as a whole.

Following these best practices and participating in the Copilot community will not only help you get better at using Microsoft Copilot, but it will also help it get better over time. Accept the idea of working together, use the community's knowledge, and start a journey of always learning and getting better with Copilot!

CHAPTER 12

COPILOT TIPS AND TRICKS

Here are some cool tips and tricks for getting the most out of Microsoft Copilot:

1. **Utilize Specific Prompts**: It is preferable to provide Copilot with cues that are both explicit and specific rather than making generic requests. This allows Copilot to better grasp what it is that you require and to generate solutions that are more helpful. Do not simply ask for assistance with functions in general if you are looking for assistance with a specific function, for instance. Be explicit about the task you are attempting to accomplish as well as the language you are using on the computer.

2. **Experiment with Different Languages**: It is possible to use Copilot with a variety of different computer languages. You can improve your ability to write code by experimenting with a variety of computer languages and seeing how Copilot responds to them. It's possible that you could acquire new approaches to problem-solving or a deeper understanding of how various languages function.

3. **Explore Advanced Features**: The code completion feature is simply one of the many features that Copilot offers. Among the capabilities that you should look into are code restructuring, code generation from notes, and clever code concepts that are dependent on context. It is important that you learn how to utilize these tools so that you can improve the quality of your code and make writing easier.

4. **Customize Copilot Settings**: You are able to modify certain settings for Copilot so that it can make decisions that are tailored to your requirements. In the options menu, you have the ability to make adjustments to items like the code style you have selected, the computer language, and the suggested modes. If you make any little adjustments to these parameters, you may find that Copilot better meets your requirements.

5. **Provide Feedback**: If the ideas that Copilot has provided do not satisfy your requirements or if you discover errors, you should provide feedback. In this way, Copilot is able to improve over time making it more likely that it will generate better ideas in the future. By using the feedback tool in Copilot or by participating in group chats, you will have the opportunity to communicate your ideas and views regarding how things could be improved.

6. **Collaborate with Copilot**: While participating in pair programming or code review sessions, Copilot can be an extremely helpful collaborator. Through the use of Copilot, you are able to generate more ideas, verify that modifications to the code are successful, and experiment with various approaches to problem-solving. When you collaborate with Copilot, you are able to devise codification strategies that are superior and more inventive overall.

7. **Stay Updated**: There are frequent updates made to Copilot by Microsoft in order to improve it, add new features and correct errors. When you want to learn about the most recent changes, you should pay attention to official announcements, release notes, and group conversations. By upgrading to the most recent version, you will be able to take advantage of the most recent enhancements and features.

8. **Practice Responsible Coding**: Copilot is capable of writing code in a short amount of time; however, it is essential to read and comprehend the code that it writes. The act of reviewing the ideas provided by Copilot, ensuring that they are correct, and ensuring that they are compatible with the requirements of your project and the coding standards are all examples of responsible coding.

Implementing these tips and tricks into your work will help you get the most out of Microsoft Copilot and improve your writing experience. To become a better coder, try new things, look into things, and work with Copilot.

Advanced Usage Techniques

Here are some advanced ways to use Microsoft Copilot that will make your experience better:

1. **Contextual Awareness**: What you mention in the inquiry and the code are the two factors that determine how well Copilot works. You will be able to benefit from this if you provide a backdrop that is both clear and comprehensive. If you use notes, variable names, and function explanations, Copilot will have an easier time understanding the code you created. In the event that you provide Copilot with additional information, its suggestions will be more accurate and helpful.

2. **Code Generation from Comments**: In order to generate code, Copilot may make use of the comments that you write. Utilizing this function to its full potential can be accomplished by writing thorough notes that outline your objectives or

requirements. Once you have left these remarks, Copilot will use them to create code snippets that are tailored to match the objectives that you have specified. When it comes to sketching out the criteria for input and output, defining the phases of a program, or writing out sophisticated logic, this can be an exceptionally beneficial tool.

3. **Refactoring Assistance**: Code restructuring jobs can be made easier with the assistance of Copilot, which provides suggestions for improving existing code. When you make changes to the code, you should provide Copilot with little sections of the code that you want to improve or optimize. If this is the case, then Copilot can provide you with a variety of options for implementing your code, ways to enhance its performance, or ways to restructure it in a manner that makes it more effective, simpler to read, and simpler to administer.

4. **Intelligent Code Completion**: More than just coming up with ideas for code completion, Copilot is capable of this. You should experiment with more difficult scenarios, such as developing entire functions or classes with the assistance of Copilot. You have the option of requesting that Copilot create complete code structures according to your requirements, rather than simply finishing short sections of code. In this way, you may speed up the writing process and reduce the amount of work you have to complete by hand.

5. **Exploratory Programming**: Utilizing Copilot is a great option for you if you want to engage in creative writing or create a prototype. For the purpose of putting ideas and theories to the test or experimenting with various approaches to problem-solving, you can easily create code snippets. The rapid code production capabilities of Copilot can be of assistance in agile software development and make it simpler to test ideas in a shorter amount of time.

6. **Language Agnostic Exploration**: Although it is particularly adept at creating code in well-known computer languages, Copilot is also capable of comprehending pseudocode and descriptions written in a language that is more widely used. Your coding jobs can be described in either pseudocode or plain English, depending on your preference. The next step is to examine how well Copilot comprehends them and utilizes them to generate code. When it comes to thinking about algorithms or putting up general design ideas, this can be extremely helpful.

7. **Customization and Personalization**: Examine the settings and customization options that are available in Copilot in order to make it behave in the manner that you choose. You can modify options such as your chosen code style, level of language understanding, and advice modes to make them more suitable for your workflow and writing style requirements. There are modifications that you may apply to Copilot in order to make it more helpful and effective for your requirements.

You can use Microsoft Copilot as a strong ally on your coding journey if you learn these advanced methods. They will help you solve difficult problems, speed up your work, and open up new opportunities in software development. Try new things with Copilot and push the limits of what it can do to get the most out of it.

Optimizing Code Generation

To optimize code generation in Microsoft Copilot, you have to use different methods to make sure that the code it makes meets your needs for speed, readability, and usefulness.

Here are some ways to make code creation with Copilot work better:

1. **Provide Clear and Specific Prompts**: It is imperative that you ensure that your cues are as precise and specific as possible while you are communicating with Copilot. Include any specifics or limits that are relevant, and make it crystal clear what it is that you want the code to accomplish. This assists Copilot in determining what it is that you want to perform and provides you with improved ideas for code.

2. **Leverage Contextual Information**: Through the addition of notes, variable names, and function descriptions to your code, you may provide Copilot with valuable context. Copilot is able to better comprehend the reasoning and logic behind your code as a result of this, which enables it to generate ideas that are more appropriate for the circumstances. In addition, if you are working on a particular job or project, you should inform Copilot about the requirements, specifications, and coding norms associated with the project.

3. **Iteratively Refine Suggestions**: The majority of the time, Copilot will provide you with more than one idea for each inquiry. You may put this to good use by continuously working to improve the code that you have now developed. You ought to begin with the first choice, and then modify it so that it aligns with your

preferences and requirements. This technique of continuous improvement gives you the ability to modify the code that is created so that it conforms to your objectives and how you typically write code.

4. **Review and Validate Generated Code**: You should carefully examine and validate the code that you have generated before adding it to your project. This will ensure that the code is correct, that it functions well, and that it adheres to the standards for coding. It is important to pay great attention to details such as the structure of the code, the naming of variables, the handling of errors, and the implementation of speed-enhancing techniques. Additionally, the code that was written should be tested in some scenarios to identify and resolve any issues or edge cases that may arise.

5. **Customize Copilot Settings**: Examine the settings and customization options that are available in Copilot to make it behave in the manner that you choose. You can modify options such as your chosen code style, level of language understanding, and advice modes to make them more suitable for your workflow and writing style requirements. To make the code changes that Copilot produces more useful and better, customization of the program can be helpful.

6. **Provide Feedback**: If Copilot writes code that doesn't meet your needs or goals, let it know. This will help it get better over time at being accurate and useful. You can use Copilot's comments feature to point out mistakes, suggest ways to make things better, or give more information for future ideas. Your opinion is very important for improving Copilot's tools and making it work better.

You can get the most out of Microsoft Copilot's code output by using these optimization methods. This will speed up your development process, make writing code easier, and make you more productive overall.

Handling Common Issues

There are some usual problems that Microsoft Copilot may have, but it is a powerful tool anyway.

Here are some successful ways to deal with these problems:

1. **Slow Response or Loading Times**:
   - **Check your internet connection:** For Copilot to work properly, you need a stable internet link. If your internet link is slow or unreliable, Copilot might not respond as quickly.
   - **Close unnecessary applications:** Running a lot of programs at once can slow down Copilot and use up system resources. Close any computer tabs or programs that you don't need to make room for Copilot.

2. **Inaccurate or Irrelevant Suggestions**:
   - **Provide clear and specific prompts:** If Copilot does not have sufficient knowledge to comprehend your requirements, it may come up with inappropriate suggestions. To assist Copilot in coming up with better ideas, you should ask it questions that are clear and detailed, and provide it with a lot of background information.
   - **Use iterative refinement:** In the event that Copilot provides you with suggestions that aren't quite correct, you should provide feedback and alter the request to continuously improve the suggestions. This may assist Copilot in learning and improving its performance over time.

3. **Code Quality Concerns**:
   - **Review and validate generated code:** Before incorporating the code that Copilot generates into your project, you should always check and make sure that it is running properly. It is important to keep an eye on aspects such as readability, speed, and adhering to the principles of the code. Make any necessary modifications or enhancements to the code to guarantee that it satisfies your requirements.
   - **Customize Copilot settings:** To accommodate your preferences and the way you write code; you can adjust the settings for Copilot. The quality of the code that is created can be improved by ensuring that the concepts that Copilot provides are in line with your objectives.

4. **Technical Errors or Crashes**:
   - **Refresh the page:** If you experience technical difficulties or crashes while using Copilot, you can try reloading the page or restarting your browser. There are

times when this can resolve issues that are just temporary and are brought on by flaws in the browser or difficulties connecting to the network.

- **Clear browser cache and cookies:** Getting rid of stored data that might be causing mistakes or conflicts by clearing your browser's cache and cookies can help fix several technical issues.
- **Report the issue:** If you keep getting errors or crashes, let Microsoft or the Copilot group know about it. Give as much information as you can about the problem, such as any error messages or signs you saw, so that the problem can be found and fixed.

5. **Privacy and Security Concerns**:
   - **Review privacy settings**: Learn the privacy settings of Copilot and check to see that they are configured to satisfy your requirements and the standards you have established for security. By reading the privacy policy of Microsoft, you will learn how the company collects, uses, and protects the information you provide when you use Copilot.
   - **Exercise caution with sensitive information:** Don't give Copilot private or sensitive information, especially when working with secret code or private data. When you share code snippets or project information in public places or files, you should be aware of the possible security risks.

By using these tips, you can easily fix common problems that come up when using Microsoft Copilot, making your writing experience faster and more productive.

CHAPTER 13

TROUBLESHOOTING GUIDE

Here's a comprehensive troubleshooting guide to help you address common issues that may arise while using Microsoft Copilot:

1. **Slow Response or Loading Times**:

Make sure your internet connection is stable and fast. When the internet is slow, Copilot may not respond as quickly. You could also try reloading the page or starting your computer over. Closing computer tabs or apps that you don't need can also help speed things up.

2. **Inaccurate or Irrelevant Suggestions**:

Provide Copilot with specific directions, as well as detailed information about your goals. You may help Copilot learn and improve over time by providing feedback and adjusting the way you ask it questions if it makes mistakes.

3. **Code Quality Concerns**:

Before adding the resulting code to your project, double-check that it works. Make sure that the code is simple to read, runs quickly, and adheres to the writing principles. You can alter the settings of Copilot to meet your coding style and inclinations.

4. **Technical Errors or Crashes**:

To resolve short-term issues, reload the page or restart your computer. It may also help to delete your browser's history and cookies. If the problem persists, notify Microsoft support or the Copilot group, providing detailed information about the error.

5. **Privacy and Security Concerns**:

Check Copilot's privacy settings to make sure they match your needs. Do not give Copilot private or sensitive information, especially in public files or groups. Tell Microsoft about any worries you have about privacy or security.

6. **Integration Issues with Code Editors**:

Make sure that Copilot is properly linked to your IDE or code editor. Check for updates or add-ons that might be needed for smooth integration. If problems still happen, look at your code editor's instructions or help materials.

7. **Compatibility Issues with Programming Languages or Frameworks**:

Check to see if Copilot works with the programming languages and frameworks you're using. It's best to check for changes or patches that might fix problems with compatibility. You could let Microsoft know that you want them to support more languages or platforms by sending them comments.

8. **Performance Degradation Over Time**:

Update both Copilot and your code editor regularly to make sure you have the newest features and better speed. Copilot's speed can be kept up over time by clearing the cache and leftover files and making the best use of the system's resources.

9. **Lack of Documentation or Support Resources**:

Investigate Microsoft's official assistance and publications for Copilot. These may include frequently asked questions (FAQs), tutorials, and troubleshooting advice. Joining forums, discussion groups, or social networking platforms allows you to ask for advice and share your experiences with other Copilot users.

If you follow these steps for fixing common problems, you should be able to get the most out of Microsoft Copilot and be more productive and efficient in your writing tasks.

Key Terms and Concepts Related to Microsoft Copilot

To get a better grasp of Microsoft Copilot, you need to become familiar with some of its most important terms and ideas.

These are some of the most important words and ideas in Microsoft Copilot:

1. **Microsoft Copilot**: Microsoft Copilot is a code completion tool powered by AI developed by Microsoft and OpenAI. It uses machine learning models that have been taught on a vast amount of code to help developers write code faster by

giving them suggestions and auto-completions that are relevant to the present context.

2. **AI Programming Assistant**: Microsoft Copilot is sometimes called an AI programming aid. It uses powerful AI algorithms to look for patterns in code, figure out what the code is about, and make code ideas as developers write code in real time.

3. **Code Completion**: This is when a writer puts in a code editor and gets suggestions for code snippets, function names, variable names, and other things. Microsoft Copilot can intelligently complete code, which makes workers more productive by giving them accurate and relevant ideas based on the current situation.

4. **Machine Learning Models**: Microsoft Copilot understands computer languages, how to code, and typical coding patterns by using machine learning models that have been trained on massive volumes of code repositories. These models are constantly updated and enhanced to make Copilot more accurate and useful.

5. **Natural Language Processing (NLP)**: NLP is a field of AI that tries to understand and use human words. NLP methods are used by Microsoft Copilot to understand the natural language prompts that developers use and make code ideas based on what they mean.

6. **Prompt**: A prompt is a request or command that a coder sends to Microsoft Copilot to generate code suggestions. The prompts can be written in standard English, small chunks of code, or particular programming jobs.

7. **Code Generation**: This is the process of instantaneously generating code segments or snippets based on what a developer types in. Microsoft Copilot helps create code since it gives you ideas on how to finish writing code, put methods into action, or construct entire functions or classes.

8. **Contextual Understanding**: Microsoft Copilot can grasp the variables, functions, and other code that is being written in the context of the current code. Because Copilot understands more about the circumstance, it may provide better, more valuable code ideas targeted to the current work.

9. **GitHub Integration**: Microsoft Copilot integrates with GitHub, a popular code storage platform. When developers are working on GitHub files, they can use Copilot directly from the code editor. This allows them to easily collaborate and produce code.

10. **Privacy and Data Security**: Because Microsoft Copilot reads code from many places, including public files; privacy and data security are important things to think about. Microsoft has put in place privacy and data protection means to make sure that user data stays safe and private while they use Copilot.

By knowing these important terms and ideas, developers will be able to make better use of Microsoft Copilot to improve their writing skills and output.

Frequently Asked Questions (FAQs)

What is the real use case for Microsoft Copilot 365 in businesses?

Adding AI-powered support to all Microsoft 365 apps via Microsoft Copilot 365 increases company productivity and facilitates collaboration. It automates typical tasks, creates content, and provides insights, making it particularly useful for creating documents, sending emails, and analyzing data.

How does GitHub Copilot assist developers in coding?

Google Code GitHub Copilot is an AI pair programmer that provides both code fragments and whole routines in real-time. It learns from the massive quantity of code on GitHub to help developers write code faster and with fewer errors. This increases their productivity and improves the quality of the code they create.

What are the benefits of Copilot for finance professionals?

Finance professionals may utilize Copilot's AI-powered insights and automation tools to analyze financial data, create reports, and make forecasts. These tools assist you in making wise decisions, maximizing your financial strategy, and completing your financial responsibilities more efficiently.

Can Microsoft Copilot 365 be used in education?

Microsoft Copilot 365 can assist teachers and students in creating content, developing learning tools, and managing administrative activities, all of which can be extremely beneficial to the educational sector. It simplifies document creation and provides important information derived from educational data.

How does GitHub Copilot adapt to different programming languages?

Google Code GitHub A lot of different programming languages can be used with Copilot. It uses what the developer says to suggest code in the language that is being used. This makes it a useful tool for software development projects that use a variety of technology stacks.

What specific features does Copilot offer to the healthcare industry?

Copilot can assist healthcare workers with data analysis, patient records management, and medical report writing. It employs AI to quickly evaluate healthcare data, providing users with insights and managing regular chores to improve patient care and operations.

How does Microsoft Copilot 365 integrate with other Microsoft applications?

Word, Excel, PowerPoint, and Outlook can all work with Microsoft Copilot 365. It adds AI-powered help right into these apps, making them more useful by adding features like help with writing, data analysis, and email management.

Is GitHub Copilot suitable for beginner programmers?

Yes, GitHub Copilot can be useful for folks who are new to coding. Real-time feedback and code samples enable new developers to learn faster and better grasp coding trends and best practices.

How can finance industries leverage AI like Copilot for risk management?

AI tools like Copilot can be used in the finance industry to look at huge amounts of financial data, find patterns, and guess what the next big trend will be. This helps with risk management by giving information that is used to measure risk, come up with ways to lower it, and make decisions.

Does Microsoft Copilot 365 have applications in project management?

Microsoft Copilot 365 can make handling projects easier by automatically making reports, keeping track of schedules, and helping to make project papers. It works with Microsoft Teams and Planner, which lets you work together and keep track of tasks.

Can GitHub Copilot contribute to open-source projects?

Google Code GitHub Copilot can help developers working on open-source projects by offering ways to add to or improve the code. However, volunteers should look over these ideas to make sure they are correct and follow the project's rules.

What role does Copilot play in the legal industry?

Copilot can help legal professionals automate paperwork, conduct case studies, and handle legal files. AI-powered systems can write legal papers based on templates and previous cases. This speeds up legal research and writing.

How does Copilot for Finance improve financial forecasting?

Copilot for Finance leverages AI to enhance financial forecasting by analyzing historical financial data and current market trends. This advanced analysis enables the generation of accurate predictions, which are critical for effective budget planning and informed decision-making. Key benefits include:

- **Data-Driven Insights**: AI algorithms assess vast amounts of financial data to identify patterns and trends, offering reliable forecasts.

- **Predictive Analytics**: By utilizing predictive models, Copilot for Finance provides businesses with actionable insights, helping to anticipate future financial performance.

- **Improved Budget Planning**: Accurate forecasts aid in creating realistic budgets, ensuring better allocation of resources and financial stability.

- **Informed Decision-Making**: Businesses can make strategic decisions based on comprehensive data analysis, reducing risks and capitalizing on opportunities.

Can Microsoft Copilot 365 assist in creating multilingual documents?

Yes, Microsoft Copilot 365 facilitates the creation of multilingual documents through its translation and language support features. This capability streamlines global communication and document preparation for businesses, offering the following advantages:

- **Translation Services**: Automatically translates text into multiple languages, making it easier to produce documents for a global audience.

- **Writing Assistance**: Provides writing help in various languages, ensuring that the content is not only accurately translated but also culturally appropriate.

- **Efficiency**: Reduces the time and effort needed to create multilingual documents, enhancing productivity.

- **Consistency**: Maintains consistency in terminology and style across different languages, improving the quality and professionalism of documents.

How does GitHub Copilot ensure the security of the code it generates?

GitHub Copilot enhances coding efficiency by suggesting code based on publicly available repositories and its training data. However, developers are responsible for ensuring the security of the generated code by:

- **Code Review**: Thoroughly review the suggested code to identify and address any potential security vulnerabilities.

- **Best Practices**: Ensuring the code follows best practices for security, including input validation, proper authentication, and secure data handling.

- **Testing**: Conduct rigorous testing, including security testing, to verify the integrity and safety of the code.

- **Awareness**: Staying informed about common security threats and how to mitigate them, as Copilot's suggestions may sometimes need adjustments to meet specific security standards.

What is Microsoft Copilot used for?

Microsoft Copilot is an AI-powered assistant integrated into various Microsoft applications to enhance productivity and efficiency. It helps users perform tasks more effectively by providing intelligent suggestions and automation.

What are the practical uses of Copilot?

Microsoft Copilot can be used for a variety of tasks, including:

- **Writing Emails**: Provides suggestions and drafts for email responses.

- **Creating Documents**: Assists in drafting, editing, and formatting documents.

- **Writing Code**: Offers code snippets and suggestions for developers.

- **Data Analysis**: Helps analyze and visualize data in applications like Excel.

- **Automating Repetitive Tasks**: Automates routine tasks to save time and effort.

Is Microsoft Copilot worth it?

For users who frequently use Microsoft platforms, Microsoft Copilot can significantly enhance productivity and efficiency, making it a worthwhile investment. Its ability to streamline various tasks and provide intelligent assistance can lead to time savings and improved output quality.

How is Copilot different from ChatGPT?

- **Integration**: Copilot is specifically designed to work within Microsoft products and leverages their unique features and capabilities.

- **Functionality**: While Copilot focuses on tasks related to Microsoft applications, ChatGPT is a general-purpose AI language model that can be used for a wide range of applications, from conversation to content creation.

Can Microsoft Copilot create images?

Creating images is not a primary function of Microsoft Copilot. However, it is continually evolving and expanding its features, which may include some basic image-related capabilities in the future.

How do I use Microsoft Copilot in Word?

To use Microsoft Copilot in Word:

- Access it through the menu or a dedicated pane within Word.

- Enter requests or commands directly into your document to receive suggestions, formatting help, or content generation.

When can we start using Microsoft Copilot?

The availability of Microsoft Copilot depends on Microsoft's rollout schedule. It may require certain accounts or subscriptions to access, so staying updated with Microsoft's announcements and updates is essential.

How do I get the most out of Microsoft Copilot?

- **Explore Features**: Familiarize yourself with all the features Copilot offers.

- **Utilize for Various Tasks**: Use it for different tasks like drafting emails, analyzing data, and automating workflows.

- **Customize Settings**: Adjust its settings to better fit your routine and specific needs.

- **Stay Updated**: Keep up with updates and new features to continuously enhance your productivity.

How do I use Copilot in Windows?

Copilot can be used on Windows through built-in programs like Office 365, which helps with Word, Excel, and Outlook, among others.

How do I use Copilot in Outlook?

Through simple orders or prompts, Outlook's Copilot helps you write letters, summarize threads, and keep track of your schedule.

What is the difference between Microsoft Copilot and GitHub Copilot?

Microsoft Copilot is meant to make Microsoft apps more productive in general, while GitHub Copilot is meant to help developers on the GitHub platform by suggesting code.

Can I use Microsoft Copilot for free?

Windows 10 It's possible that Copilot will need a membership to Microsoft 365 or certain Microsoft services. Free may only be available for a limited time or with certain deals.

Is Copilot available for Excel?

Yes, Copilot is available for Excel and can be used to analyze data, make formulas, and automate spreadsheets.

Is Microsoft Copilot part of Office 365?

Because Microsoft Copilot is built into Office 365, the suite's apps can do more with AI-powered features.

Does Microsoft Copilot have an API?

As Microsoft continues to enhance its offerings, the availability and specifics of an API for Microsoft Copilot may change. To get the most current information, it's recommended to check Microsoft's official documentation and updates.

What is Google's answer to Microsoft Copilot?

Google offers various AI-driven tools and features within its Workspace suite, designed to enhance productivity and collaboration, serving as a counterpart to Microsoft Copilot.

Is Microsoft Copilot generative AI?

Yes, Microsoft Copilot utilizes generative AI technologies, such as language models like ChatGPT, to assist users in creating content and automating tasks.

What is the role of the Large Language Model in Copilot for Microsoft 365?

Large Language Models (LLMs) in Copilot for Microsoft 365 take user input and generate contextually relevant, human-like text, facilitating seamless interactions with Microsoft 365 applications.

How do LLMs understand user queries in Copilot?

LLMs analyze the context and subject matter of queries to generate appropriate and coherent responses, enhancing the overall user experience.

What makes LLMs essential for AI interactions in Microsoft 365?

LLMs are crucial for AI interactions in Microsoft 365 because they enable the AI to understand and respond intelligently to user inputs, making the interactions more natural and effective.

How do LLMs enhance the user experience in Microsoft 365?

By providing sophisticated language understanding, LLMs enhance productivity and efficiency, making tasks easier and faster to complete within Microsoft 365 applications.

Can LLMs adapt to different user needs in Copilot?

Yes, LLMs can generate responses tailored to the user's specific context and past interactions, providing more personalized assistance.

What types of tasks can LLMs assist within Microsoft 365?

LLMs can assist with a variety of work-related tasks, such as drafting emails, creating documents, generating spreadsheets, and analyzing data.

How does Copilot ensure LLM responses are relevant?

Copilot employs advanced algorithms to ensure that the responses generated by LLMs are contextually appropriate and aligned with the user's intentions.

Do LLMs in Copilot improve over time?

Yes, LLMs learn from interactions and improve their performance and responsiveness over time.

Can LLMs in Copilot understand multiple languages?

LLMs are designed to handle and understand multiple languages, making them accessible to a global user base.

How secure are LLM interactions in Copilot?

Microsoft prioritizes security, ensuring that interactions with LLMs in Copilot are private and secure.

Do LLMs in Copilot require internet access?

Yes, LLMs in Copilot require internet access as they rely on cloud computing to process and deliver responses.

Can LLMs handle specialized tasks within Microsoft 365 apps?

LLMs are capable of managing specialized tasks by leveraging app-specific features and knowledge.

How user-friendly is the interface for interacting with LLMs in Copilot?

The interface for interacting with LLMs in Copilot is designed to be intuitive and user-friendly, facilitating easy engagement.

Will LLMs in Copilot replace human input?

While LLMs significantly enhance productivity, they are designed to complement human creativity and decision-making, not replace it.

How does Copilot with LLMs contribute to collaboration in Microsoft 365?

Copilot with LLMs streamlines collaboration by automating tedious tasks and enabling efficient and clear communication among users within Microsoft 365.

CONCLUSION

Microsoft Copilot is the first AI-powered efficiency tool, and it marks the start of a new era of work and invention. Because it has so many uses for developers, business people, and security teams, it is a major force in the constantly changing world of technology.

In the fields of artificial intelligence and computing, Microsoft Copilot is a huge step forward. Modern machine learning techniques are used in this ground-breaking tool to help developers write high-quality code quickly and easily. By using Copilot's features, developers can get a lot more done and focus on the more creative parts of programming while the tool takes care of the boring and repetitive tasks.

More than that, Copilot will only get stronger and better over time because it can learn from its exchanges with developers. Because Microsoft Copilot can be used in all of Microsoft's apps, it will also change how companies use their workers. Because of this, Microsoft Copilot is about to change the way workers work and will be very important in shaping the future of software development.

INDEX